Five Minute Bread

Five Minute Bread

The Discovery that Revolutionises
Home Baking

Jeff Hertzberg and Zoë François

10 9 8 7 6 5 4 3 2 1

Ebury Press, an imprint of Ebury Publishing,
20 Vauxhall Bridge Road,
London, SW1V 2SA

Ebury Press is part of the Penguin Random House group
whose addresses can be found at global.penguinrandomhouse.com

Penguin
Random House
UK

First published by Ebury Press in 2010
This paperback edition published in 2018

www.penguin.co.uk

A CIP catalogue record for this book is available from the British Library

Design: Lottie Crumblehome
Copyeditor: Jane Banforth
Illustrator: Emma Löfström

ISBN: 9781529102956

Printed and bound in Great Britain by Clays Ltd, St Ives PLC

Penguin Random House is committed to a sustainable future for
our business, our readers and our planet. This book is made from
Forest Stewardship Council® certified paper.

With love to Laura, Rachel and Julia,
who fear nothing and love to bake.
J.H.

To Graham, Henri and Charlie,
my inspiration in the kitchen and in life.
Z.F.

CONTENTS

———

THE SECRET

Mix Enough Dough for Several Loaves and Store It in the Fridge

It is so easy to have freshly baked bread when you want it with only five minutes a day of active effort. First, mix the ingredients from our recipe into a container all at once, and then let them sit for two hours. Now you are ready to shape and bake the bread, or you can refrigerate the dough and use it over the next couple of weeks. Yes, weeks! You've prepared enough dough for many loaves. When you want fresh-baked crusty bread, take a piece of the dough from the container and shape it into a loaf. Let it rise for 20 minutes or more and then bake. Your house will smell like a bakery and your family and friends will love you for it.

PREFACE

Early childhood music class may be one of the more unlikely places for co-authors to meet. I met Zoë amidst toddlers, circle games and xylophones, and while the kids played, there was time for the grown-ups to talk. Zoë told me that she was a pastry chef and baker who'd been trained at the Culinary Institute of America (CIA).

What a fortuitous coincidence. I wasn't a food professional at all, but I'd been tinkering for years with easy methods for making home-made bread. We chatted about the challenges of re-creating authentic baguettes without French flour ('You can't? Uh, yeah, I knew that.'). I told her about a recipe I'd been trying to develop for years to create artisan breads at home while investing minimal time. The secret: use pre-mixed, high-moisture stored dough. It was promising, but it needed lots of work. This was a job for a professional baker.

I knew I had to get her to try the bread to convince her that she ought to join me in this project (and maybe more important, that involvement with five minute yeast bread wouldn't turn her into a culinary laughing stock). This woman was a baker whose food at Minneapolis restaurants had been reviewed as 'endlessly delicious . . . the best in town . . . appealing, inventive and flat-out gorgeous. . . .' Maybe she had lower standards for bread than for dessert.

Luckily for me, she loved the bread, and she was willing to work on developing a book with me. And she had an idea for how to use the same approach to make pastries. Zoë created rich, sweet doughs from the basic recipe and turned them into a menu of fantastic sweet breads, pastries, rolls and even doughnuts. I couldn't have anticipated this in a million years. I was startled at how easily stored yeast dough could be adapted for dessert (although Zoë knew all along that it would work).

I was trained as a scientist, not as a chef. That might have helped in developing a completely new process for home-made bread for amateurs, but I never could have brought the recipes to this level without the rigorous standards and creative repertoire of a professional. Our approach produces fantastic home-made loaves without the enormous time investment required in the traditional artisanal method.

Our goal in *Five Minute Bread* is to help home bakers make great daily breads and pastries but still have a life outside the kitchen. And most important, for them to have fun while doing it. If you worry about the bread, it won't taste as good. For additional tips, photos and videos, please visit www.fiveminutebread.com.

HOW TO MAKE BREAD IN FIVE MINUTES A DAY

Refrigerating Pre-Mixed Home-Made Dough

Like most kids, my brother and I loved sweets, so dessert was our favourite time of day. We'd sit in the kitchen, devouring frosted supermarket doughnuts.

'Those are too sweet,' my grandmother would say. 'Me, I'd rather have a piece of good rye bread, with cheese on it.'

Munch, munch, munch. Our mouths were full; we could not respond.

'It's better than cake,' she'd say.

There's a certain solidarity among kids gorging on sweets, but secretly, I knew she was right. I could finish half a loaf of very fresh, very crisp rye bread by myself, with or without butter (unlike my grandmother, I considered cheese to be a distraction from perfect rye bread). The right stuff came from a little bakery on Horace Harding Boulevard in Queens. The shop itself was nondescript, but the breads were eastern European masterpieces. The crust of the rye bread was crisp, thin and caramelised brown. The interior crumb was moist, dense and chewy, and bursting with tangy yeast, rye and wheat flavours. It made great toast, too – and yes, it was better than cake.

The handmade bread was available all over New York City, and it wasn't a rarefied delicacy. Everyone knew what it was and took it for granted. It was not a stylish addition to affluent lifestyles; it was a simple comfort food brought here by modest immigrants.

I left New York in the late 1980s, and assumed that the corner bread shops would always be there, waiting for me, whenever I came back to visit. But I was wrong. As people lost interest in making a second stop after the supermarket just for bread, the shops gradually faded away. By 1990, the ubiquitous corner shops turning out great eastern, central and southern European breads with crackling crusts were no longer so ubiquitous.

Great European breads, handmade by artisans, were still available, but they'd become part of the serious (and seriously expensive) food phenomenon that had swept the country. The bread bakery was no longer on every corner – now it was a destination. And nobody's grandmother would ever have paid six dollars for a loaf of bread.

I'd fly back to New York and wander the streets, bereft (well, not really). 'My shop' on Horace Harding Boulevard had changed hands several times by 1990, and the bread, being made only once a day, was dry and didn't really have a lot of flavour. I even became convinced that we could get better bagels in Minneapolis – and from a supermarket. Things were that grim.

So Zoë and I decided to do something about it. *Five Minute Bread* is our attempt to help people re-create the great ethnic breads of years past, in their own homes, without investing serious time in the process. Using our straightforward, fast and easy recipes, anyone will be able to create artisan bread and pastry at home with minimal equipment. Our first problem was: who has time to make bread every day?

After years of experimentation, it turns out that we do, and with a method as fast as ours, you can, too. We solved the time problem and produced top-quality artisan loaves without a bread machine. We worked out the master recipes during busy years of career transition and starting families (our kids now delight in the pleasures of home-baked bread). Our lightning-fast method lets us find the time to bake great bread every day. We developed this method to recapture the daily artisan bread experience without further crunching our limited time – and it works!

Traditional breads need a lot of attention, especially if you want to use a 'starter' for that natural, tangy taste. Starters need to be cared for, with water and flour replenished from time to time. Dough needs to be kneaded until resilient, set to rise, punched down, allowed to rise again. There are boards and pans and utensils galore to be washed, some of which can't go into the dishwasher. Very few busy people can go through this every day, if ever. Even if your friends are all food fanatics, when was the last time you had home-made bread at a dinner party?

What about bread machines? The machines solve the time problem and turn out uniformly decent loaves, but unfortunately, the crust is soft and dull-flavoured, and without tangy flavour in the crumb (unless you use and maintain a time-consuming sourdough starter).

What We Don't Have to Do:
Steps from Traditional Baking that We Omitted

---

1. Mix a new batch of dough every time we want to make bread

2. Prove yeast

3. Knead dough

4. Cover formed loaves

5. Rest and rise the loaves in a draught-free location – it doesn't matter!

6. Fuss over doubling or tripling of dough volume

7. Punch down and re-rise

8. Poke rising loaves to be sure they've proved by leaving indentations

Now you know why it only takes 5 minutes a day, not including resting and baking time.

Start a morning batch before work, bake the first loaf before dinner

———————————

Here's a convenient way to get fresh bread on the table for dinner. Mix up a full batch of dough before breakfast and store it in the fridge. The lukewarm water you used to mix the dough will provide enough heat to allow the yeast to do its thing over the eight hours till you're home. When you walk in the door, cloak (see page 46 for details on 'cloaking') and shape the loaf and give it a quick rest, then bake as usual. Small loaves, and especially flatbreads, can be on the table in 40 minutes or less.

So we went to work. Over years, we found how to subtract the various steps that make the classic technique so time-consuming, and identified a few that couldn't be omitted.

And then, Zoë worked some pastry-chef magic: she figured out that we could use stored dough for desserts as well as for bread, applying the same ideas to sweet breads, rolls and morning breads. It all came down to one fortuitous discovery: **pre-mixed, pre-risen, high-moisture dough keeps well in the fridge.**

This is the linchpin of *Five Minute Bread*. By pre-mixing high-moisture dough (without kneading) and then storing it, daily bread baking becomes an easy activity; the only steps you do every day are shaping and baking. Other books have considered refrigerating dough, but only for a few days. Still others have omitted the kneading step, but none has tested the capacity of wet dough to be long-lived in your fridge. As our high-moisture dough ages, it takes on sourdough notes, reminiscent of the great European natural starters. When dough is mixed with adequate water (this dough is wetter than most you may have worked with), it can be stored in the fridge for up to two weeks (enriched or heavy doughs can't go that long but can be frozen instead). And kneading this kind of dough adds little to the overall product; you just don't have to do it. In fact, overhandling stored dough can limit the volume and rise that you get with our method. That, in a nutshell, is how you make artisan breads with the investment of only five minutes a day of active effort.

A one- or two-week supply of dough is made in advance and stored in the fridge. Measuring and mixing the dough takes less than 15 minutes. Kneading, as we've said, is not necessary. Every day, cut off a hunk of dough from the storage container and briefly shape it without kneading. Allow it to rest briefly on the work surface and then toss it in the oven. We don't count the rest time (20 minutes or more depending on the recipe) or baking time (usually about 30 minutes) in our five-minute-a-day calculation, since you can be doing something else while that's happening. If you bake after dinner, the bread will stay fresh for use the next day (higher moisture breads stay fresh longer), but the method is so convenient that you probably will find you can cut off some dough and bake a loaf every morning, before your day starts. If you want to have one thing you do every day that is simply perfect, this is it!

Using high-moisture, pre-mixed, pre-risen dough makes the most of the difficult, time-consuming and demanding steps in traditional bread baking completely superfluous:

1. **You don't need to make fresh dough every day to have fresh bread every day:** Stored dough makes wonderful fresh loaves. Only the shaping and baking steps are done daily, the rest has been done in advance.

2. **You don't need a 'sponge' or 'starter':** Traditional sourdough recipes require that you keep flour-water mixtures bubbling along in your fridge, with careful attention and replenishment. By storing the dough over two weeks, a subtle sourdough character gradually develops in our breads without needing to maintain sponges or starters in the fridge. With our dough storage approach, your first loaf is not exactly the same as the last. It will become more complex in flavour as the dough ages.

3. **It doesn't matter how you mix the dry and wet ingredients together:** So long as the mixture is uniform, without any dry lumps of flour, it makes no difference whether you use a spoon, a high-capacity food processor or a heavy-duty mixer. Choose based on your own convenience.

4. **You don't need to prove yeast:** Traditional recipes specify that yeast be dissolved in water (often with a little sugar) and allowed to sit for five minutes to prove that bubbles can form and the yeast is alive. But modern yeast simply doesn't fail if used before its expiry date and the baker remembers to use lukewarm, not hot water. The high-water content in our doughs further ensures that the yeast will fully hydrate and activate without a proving step. Further storage gives it plenty of time to fully ferment the dough – our approach doesn't need the head start.

5 **It isn't kneaded:** The dough can be mixed and stored in the same resealable plastic container. No wooden board is required. There should be only one container to wash, plus a spoon (or a mixer). You'll never tell the difference between breads made with kneaded and unkneaded high-moisture dough, so long as you mix to a basically uniform consistency. In our method, a very quick 'cloaking and shaping' step substitutes for kneading (see The Master Recipe, Step 5, page 47).

6. **High-moisture stored dough can't over-rise accidentally:** Remember that you're storing it long term anyway. You'll see a brisk initial rise at room temperature over two hours; then the risen dough is refrigerated for use over the next week or two. But rising longer won't be harmful; there's lots of leeway in the initial rise time.

Given these simple principles, anyone can make artisan bread at home. We'll talk about what you'll need in the Ingredients chapter (pages 21–25) and the Equipment chapter (pages 27–29). You don't need a professional baker's kitchen. After equipment, you'll learn the tips and techniques that we've taken years to accumulate (pages 31–41). Then we'll lay out the basics of our method in The Master Recipe chapter (pages 43–49), applying them to ordinary white dough and several delicious bread variations. This recipe is the model for all the others in the book. We suggest you read it first and bake some of its breads before trying anything else. You won't regret it.

Wetter is better: The wetter dough, as you'll see, is fairly slack, and offers less resistance to yeast's expanding carbon dioxide bubbles. So, despite not being replenished with fresh flour and water like a proper sourdough starter, there is still adequate rise on the work surface and in the oven.

INGREDIENTS

Here's a very practical guide to the ingredients we use to produce artisan loaves. Great breads really only require four basic ingredients: flour, water, yeast and salt. The rest is detail.

Flours and Grains

Unbleached, white plain flour: This is the staple ingredient for most of the recipes in this book.

Unbleached plain flour is our number-one choice because of its medium- (rather than high-) protein content, which in wheat is almost all gluten. Gluten is the elastic protein that sets up a network of invisible microscopic strands, allowing bread dough to trap the carbon dioxide gas produced by bread yeast. Without gluten, bread won't rise. That's why flours that contain only minimal gluten (like rye) need to be mixed with wheat flour to make a successful loaf. Traditional bread recipes stress the need to 'develop' gluten through kneading, which turns out not to be an important factor.

With a protein/gluten content at around 10 per cent in most brands, unbleached plain flour will have adequate protein to create a satisfying 'chew' (a certain resistance to the teeth), but will have a low enough protein content to prevent heaviness, which can be a problem in high-moisture artisan baking.

Don't use bleached flour. We prefer unbleached flours for their natural creamy colour, not to mention our preference for avoiding unnecessary chemicals. Even more important, bleaching removes some of the protein, and that throws off our recipes. If you use bleached flour, your dough will be too wet.

Strong flour: Strong flour has about 12 per cent protein. If you prefer extra-chewy bread, you can substitute strong flour for plain by decreasing the amount slightly (by about 35g/1¼oz for every 840g/1lb 14oz white plain flour in the recipe). For some loaves that really need to hold their shape well (like Pain d'Epí, pages 60–1), strong flour is preferred and we call for it in the recipe.

Wholemeal flour: Wholemeal flour contains both the germ and bran of wheat; both of which are healthy and tasty. Together they add a slightly bitter, nutty flavour to bread that most people enjoy. The naturally occurring oils in wheat germ prevent formation of a crackling crust, so you're going for a different type of loaf when you start increasing the proportion of wholemeal flour. In general, you can use any kind of wholemeal flour that's available to you. Stoneground wholemeal flour will be a bit coarser and more rustic. Either plain or strong wholemeal flour will work well in our recipes.

Rye flour: A variety of rye flours are available. They have varying percentages of rye bran, but the labelling generally doesn't make this clear. Be aware, though, that the very coarse-ground, high-bran products will produce a coarser, denser loaf.

Semolina flour: Semolina is a major component of some Italian breads, where it lends a beautiful yellow colour and spectacular flavour. The best semolina for bread is the finely ground 'semolina flour'.

Oats: We use rolled oats or oat flour in several recipes. It adds a wonderful hearty flavour and contributes to a toothsome texture, but it doesn't have any gluten content. So, like rye flour, it needs to be paired with plain flour to produce a loaf that rises.

Organic flours: We have to admit, we can't tell the difference from the standpoint of flavour or texture. If you like organic products, by all means use them (we often do). But they're not required, and they certainly cost more. One reason some people take up the bread-baking hobby is to be able to eat organic bread every day, as it is usually unavailable commercially or is prohibitively expensive.

Oil

When we refer to neutral-flavoured oil, this means sunflower oil, corn oil, canola oil or any oils that are not strong-flavoured (i.e. not olive oil, almond oil, etc.).

Water

We can't detect important differences between water sources. The flavours of wheat and yeast overwhelm the contribution of water to bread's flavour. We use ordinary tap water running through a home water filter, but that's only because it's what we drink at home. Assuming your own tap water tastes good enough to drink, use it filtered or unfiltered; we can't tell the difference in finished bread.

Yeast

Yeast is crucial to bread's rise, and also to its flavour. Our recipes call for plenty of yeast, in order to ensure a quick and vigorous initial rise. This is really a matter of taste, and some experienced bakers may prefer the more delicate flavour of a dough risen with less packaged yeast. Some traditionalists feel that rising the dough very slowly, with very little added yeast, builds a better flavour.

Less yeast will work for all of our recipes, but be aware that the initial rise will be slower, and the resting/rising time will also be increased. We've had good results using as little as one-quarter of the specified level of yeast (initial rising time will be much longer). Use whatever yeast is readily available; with our approach you just won't be able to tell the difference between the various national brands of yeast, nor between instant, regular, granulated, or cake yeast (though you will have to double the quantity if you use cake yeast).

The long storage time of our doughs acts as an equaliser between all of these. One strong recommendation: buy in bulk or in commercially available jars, rather than in envelopes. The envelopes are much more expensive, ounce for ounce. Between the two of us, we've had only one yeast failure in many years of baking, and it was with an outdated envelope. Excellent results can be had with bulk-purchased yeast. Just be sure it's fresh.

The real key to avoiding yeast failures is to use water that is no warmer than lukewarm (about 38°C). Even cold water will work, though rising will take much longer. Hot water kills yeast. After several days of high-moisture storage, yeasted dough begins to take on a flavour and aroma that approximates the flavour of natural sourdough starters used in many artisan breads. Sours and starters like *biga* (Italian), *levain* (French), and *poolish* (referred to in Eastern European, French, and Italian recipes) all require significant time and attention, so our books don't ask you to make them.

Modern Yeast

It almost never fails if used before its expiry date, so you do not need to wait until the yeast proves (bubbles), nor do you need to add sugar. We avoid proving yeast because it consumes five precious minutes! But it's probably a good idea to add the yeast to the water as the very first added ingredient. This hydrates the yeast and ensures that you won't get undissolved granules in the dough. Though the truth is that you don't have to wait for it to dissolve fully: some modern recipes have you mix all the dry ingredients (including yeast) together before adding liquids, and they work fine. The same is true for the salt

Salt: Adjust It To Your Taste

Neither of us is able to distinguish among salt types in baked breads – save your expensive artisanal sea salts for sprinkling over finished dishes as they come to table. We used coarse grain salt because we find it's easy to handle, but you can use fine grain salt as well; just decrease the volume by about 33%, as it packs tighter in the container and in the spoon. We love the taste of salt, so our recipes call for a fairly good dose of it – it can be adjusted downward if you like your bread less salty, or if you have health concerns that prompt you to seek out a lower-salt diet. Cutting the salt in half or less can be a good option for people who want to restrict sodium in their diet. Experiment, and see what you think.

Seeds, Nuts and Chocolate

Caraway seeds: These are so central to the flavour of many rye breads that a lot of people think that caraway is actually the flavour of the rye grain. It's not, but for us, something does seem to be missing in unseeded rye bread. The only problem you can run into with caraway seeds (or any other) is that in very old ones the internal oil may have gone rancid. Taste a few if your jar is older than a year.

Other seeds: Poppy, sesame and pumpkin seeds are featured in a number of our recipes. They occasionally turn rancid, so taste a few if your jar is older than a year.

Nuts: Store in the freezer so the oils will not go rancid. Buy them either natural or blanched.

Chocolate: Some of our enriched breads call for chocolate, either cocoa powder, a bar of chocolate or chunks. You will notice an improvement in flavour and recipe performance if you use the highest-quality chocolate available because of the purity of the ingredients. For plain chocolate, Valrhona is our favourite, but Lindt and other premium brands also work quite well. If premium chocolates are unavailable, try the recipes with your favourite supermarket brands. The premium stuff is not an absolute requirement by any means.

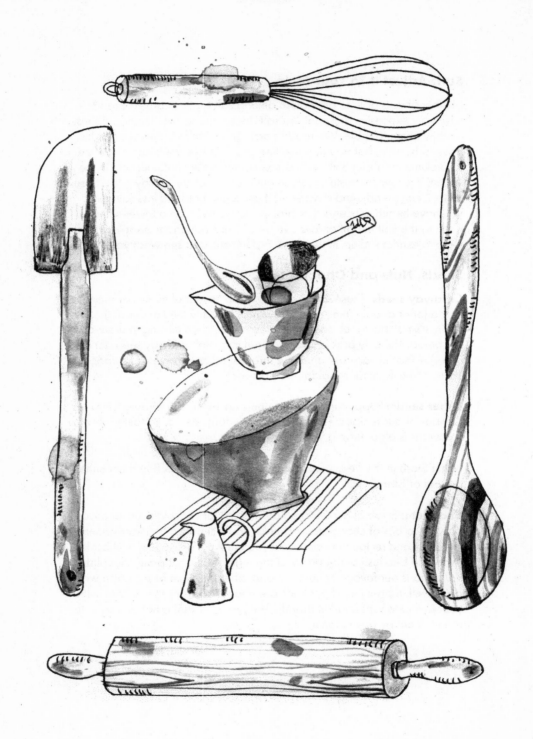

EQUIPMENT

Oven thermometer: This is one item that isn't optional; you need it to calibrate your oven to get predictable bread-baking results. A hot oven drives excess water out of wet dough, but if it's too high you'll burn the crust before fully baking the crumb (the bread's interior). Home ovens are often off by up to 20°C. With an inexpensive oven thermometer, you can be certain to get results as good as ours are. Without the thermometer, your bread-baking experiments are going to require an annoying element of trial and error.

Baking stone: For best results, you'll want a high-quality, 1cm/½in-thick baking stone (thin ones may crack within a year if used frequently). Look for a large one, preferably with a lifetime replacement guarantee against cracking. The porous stone absorbs excess moisture from your wet dough, allowing a thin, crackling, crisp crust to form; this crust is one of the key elements in artisanal baking. Free-form loaves are baked right on the stone; liberal use of polenta or flour prevents sticking. You can bake wet dough on a baking sheet or other nonporous surface, but the crust won't be as good.

A large plastic storage container with a lid: You can mix and store the dough in the same vessel and save yourself from having to wash one more item (it all figures into the five minutes a day). You need something large – a food container that holds about 5 litres/8¾ pints. If you double the quantities in our recipes (resulting in a little less than 3.6kg/8lb of dough), you'll need something in the order of 9–10 litres/16–17½ pints.

Grill tray to hold boiling water for steam: This is essential for breads intended to achieve a crackling crust and nice caramelisation. Most enriched breads (e.g. challah, brioche, etc) won't benefit from it, since the fat in their dough prevents the crackling crust.
    Warning: Do not use a glass pan to catch water for steam, or it will shatter! Occasionally oven windows has been known to crack after water has been spilled on it. To prevent this, cover the window with a towel before throwing water into the pan; remove before closing the oven door.

Pizza peel: This is a flat board with a long handle used to slide bread and pizzas onto a hot stone. Wood or metal work equally well (you can't use anything made of plastic to transfer into the oven because of the contact with a very hot baking stone). Coat liberally with polenta before putting wet dough loaves on them or they will stick to the peel and/or the stone. If you don't have a pizza peel, a flat baking sheet with no sides will do, but it will be more difficult to handle, as will a wood-chopping board.

Baking sheets and silicone mats: You may opt to bake your first bread on the baking sheet that you already have in the house. Similar results are obtained with the new non-stick, flexible silicone baking mats, which don't need to be greased and are used on top of a baking sheet (washing up is a breeze). Or, you can line your baking sheet with parchment paper, which also provides a nice non-stick surface and easy washing up. All these non-porous options give respectable results, but don't expect a crackling crust.

Loaf tins: Like baking sheets and silicone mats, loaf tins work well but don't promote the development of a great crackling crust. One word of caution about loaf tins: you must use a pan with a non-stick coating, and even then we find that a light greasing is needed. Our wet doughs will stick to traditional loaf tins no matter how much you grease and/or flour them. Non-stick loaf tins with the approximate dimensions of 23 x 10 x 7.5cm/9 × 4 × 3in work best. Fill the pan a little more than half full.

Brioche tins: Traditionally, brioche is baked either in a fluted brioche mould or in a loaf tin. The fluted mould is easy to find either online or in a kitchenware shop. They are available in several sizes, with or without a non-stick coating; and flexible silicone brioche moulds are now available.

Panettone moulds: Large ceramic ramekins or ordinary fluted brioche tins work nicely, or you can buy an authentic panettone tin, or panettone moulds made from paper.

Bread knife: A serrated bread knife is very helpful, because it does a great job cutting through fresh bread without tearing or compressing, and also because it's the best implement we've found for slashing high-moisture loaves just before baking the bread.

Cooling rack: These are the wire racks usually intended for cakes. They are very helpful in preventing the soggy bottom crust that can result when you cool bread on a plate or other non-porous surfaces.

Dough scraper: Once you start making pizza and other rolled-out flatbreads, you may want a rigid metal scraper to detach the dough when it sticks to your work surface. The dough scraper is very useful for cutting wet dough into equal portions prior to making 'ropes' for plaited loaves. It's also the only easy way to scrape excess flour and polenta off your hot stone.

Measuring spoons: Seek out a set that includes a half-tablespoon measure in addition to the usual suspects. Many of our recipes call for one and one-half tablespoons of salt and yeast. If you can't find a half-tablespoon measure, just measure out one and a half teaspoons.

Mixers and food processors. These are even easier than hand-mixing: If you're using a machine to mix dough, incorporating the flour is simple. Whether you use a machine or mix by hand, your goal is to uniformly moisten all the flour and get rid of any dry patches (you can stop at that point). It will remain sticky but should hold a free-form loaf shape when you try to form one later in the recipe. With food processors, you'll need to add the dry ingredients first, then pour in the liquids, or there'll be some leakage around the bottom.

Parchment paper: Parchment paper is a great alternative to cornmeal for preventing loaves from sticking to the pizza peel as they're slid into the oven. The paper goes right with the loaf, on to the preheated stone. Most kitchen parchment products have a silicon coating that blocks moisture transfer to the stone, so you should peel the paper off the loaf for the last third of baking. Otherwise you won't get a crispy bottom crust. One other advantage of parchment even for cookie-sheet bakers, is that it eliminates the need to grease the cookie sheet.

Pastry brushes: These look like small paintbrushes, and are used to paint cornflour wash, egg wash or water onto the surface of loaves just before baking.

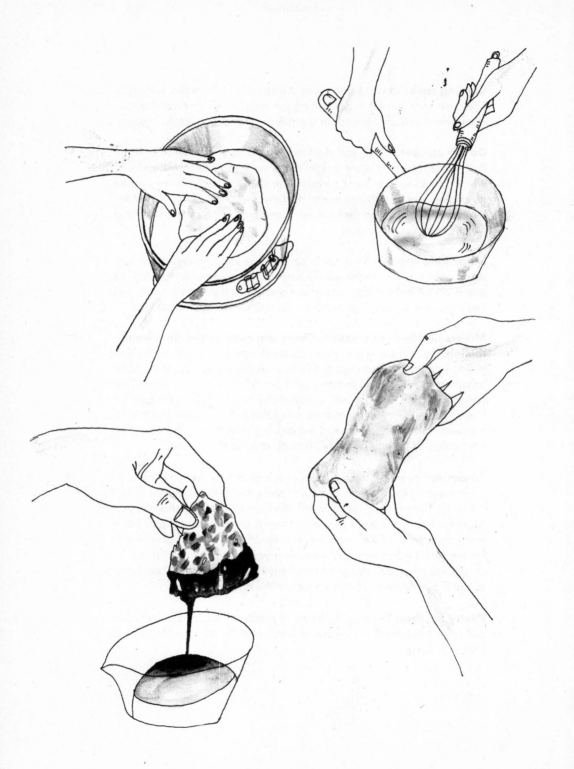

TIPS AND TECHNIQUES

This chapter will help you perfect your stored-dough, high-moisture breads. In the discussion that follows, we provide tips and techniques to achieve breads with a professional-quality crust (exterior) and crumb (interior).

Dough Moisture Content

Our recipes were carefully tested, and we arrived at the ratio of wet to dry ingredients with an eye towards creating a relatively 'slack' and wet dough. But flours can vary in their protein content, the degree to which they're compacted into their containers, and in the amount of water they've absorbed from the environment. And environment changes; in most places, humidity will fluctuate over the course of the year. All of this means that the specified dry ingredients may produce slightly variable results depending on humidity, compaction and the flour brand you're using.

If you're finding that the doughs are too stiff (especially if they don't show much rising capacity after a few days in the fridge), when making the next batches decrease the amount of flour by 35g/1¼oz. And if they're too loose and wet, and don't hold a shape well for free-form loaves, increase the amount of flour, again by 35g/1¼oz. You'll find that your overly wet dough still works better in loaf tins, where it can't spread sideways. The same is true for long-saved dough (more than ten days or so).

How to vary our recipes
based on your taste

—————————————

If you modify a recipe using **more liquid** (giving you wetter dough), you'll get...

• Larger air holes

• Desirable 'custard' interior (see opposite), can become 'gummy' if too little flour is used or too much whole grain is included

• May be difficult for free-form loaf to hold shape, may spread laterally, but will do very well in loaf tins

• Requires less resting time before baking

If you modify a recipe using **less liquid** (giving you drier dough), you'll get...

• Smaller air holes

• Difficult to achieve custard interior; interior will be drier

• Free-form loaves will hold shape well and remain high and domed

• Requires more resting time before baking

Storing Dough

In order to realise the ultimate value of our approach, and have daily artisan fresh-baked bread in only 5 minutes a day, you'll want to make enough dough to last a week or more. Your initial time investment (mixing the dough) is the most significant one, though it generally takes no more than 15 minutes. By mixing larger batches, you can spread that investment over more days of bread-making. So we really recommend mixing enough dough to last at least 7 to 10 days. For larger households, that might mean doubling, or even tripling the recipes as written in the book. Store the whole thing in a covered plastic container large enough to mix all the dough you need and accommodate the dough's rising.

'Custard' Crumb

Perfectly baked high-moisture dough can produce a delightful 'custard' crumb (interior). Wheat flour's protein is gluten, and as the gluten cooks with water, it traps some of the water, creating a chewy and moist crumb, with a shiny and moist surface seen in the larger air holes. As you adjust flour amounts for your favourite recipes, you'll find that this is an effect you can manipulate. Too much flour, and you will lose the 'custard' crumb character. Too little, and the dough will be difficult to shape and the breads gummy; this is easy to adjust. If your batch is too wet, you can work in more flour at the gluten-cloaking step, or in its storage container. If too dry, add more water, using wet hands at the shaping step.

Resting and Baking Times

All of our resting and baking times are approximate. Since loaves are formed by hand, their size will vary from loaf to loaf. There can be significant changes in resting and baking time requirements with changes in loaf size. Although large, flat loaves will bake rapidly, large, high-domed loaves will require dramatically longer baking times. So unless you're weighing out exact 450g/1lb loaves and forming the same shapes each time, your resting and baking times will vary and our listed time should be seen only as a starting point for 450g/1lb free-form loaves (675g/1½lb loaf-tin loaves). Here are some basic guidelines for varying resting and baking times and oven temperatures based on the characteristics of that day's loaf:

Increase resting and baking time if either of the following applies:
• Larger loaf
• More whole grain

Adjust baking temperature based on dough ingredients:
• Non-enriched doughs made mostly from white flour: 230°C/gas mark 8
• Egg, honey or brioche dough: 180°C/gas mark 4
• High wholemeal content (more than 50 per cent by volume): 180°C/gas mark 4

Oven preheat

Throughout the book, we specify a relatively short oven preheat (30 minutes) with the baking stone. In some ovens, and with some stones, you may find that you need a longer preheat in order to ensure that the bottom crust crisps nicely – 40 minutes should do the trick.

Varying the Grain that Covers the Pizza Peel

After a short rest, most of our breads are slid off a pizza peel directly on to a hot baking stone. Polenta is the usual 'lubricant' covering the peel and helping to slip the loaf off the peel and on to the stone. It prevents the loaf from sticking to either the pizza peel or the hot stone. But polenta is only one of many options. We tend to use polenta for the more rustic, full-flavoured loaves, and wholemeal flour for the more delicate breads, like the French baguette. Even white flour works for the same purpose in pitta and ciabatta. But coarser grains like polenta are the most 'slippery,' and fine-ground wheat flours may require a heavier coating to prevent sticking (sometimes you'll have to nudge the loaves off with a spatula or metal scraper). Mostly though, the choice of grain on the pizza peel is a matter of taste.

If you're still having trouble sliding loaves off the pizza peel, consider using parchment paper instead of polenta. The paper slides into the oven with the bread and is peeled off two-thirds of the way through baking. Most parchment products have a silicone coating that partially prevents the escape of moisture from the bottom crust into the stone, and that moisture can prevent crisping – that's the reason for peeling it off at the two-thirds point.

Underbaking Problems

Crust is hard and crispy when it emerges from the oven, but it softens as it comes to room temperature: This is most often a problem with very large breads, but it can happen with any loaf. The problem is that you've slightly underbaked the bread. The internal moisture, so high in wet dough, redistributes to the crust as the bread cools. If you haven't driven off enough water with heat, moisture will move from the interior (crumb) to the exterior (crust) and make it soft. As you gain experience, you will come to understand just how brown the loaf must be to prevent this problem with any given loaf size. We use brownness and crust firmness as our measure of 'doneness' (there will be a few blackened bits on the loaf in non-egg breads). If you have a crust that is initially crisp but softens as it cools, the bread can even be returned to the oven until you achieve the desired result.

Loaf has a soggy or gummy crumb (interior): If it's really soggy, you have an underbaking problem.
• Check your oven temperature with a thermometer.
• Make sure you are allowing the dough to rest for the full time period we've recommended.
• Your dough may benefit from being a little drier. For the next batch, increase the amount of flour by 35g/1¼oz (or decrease the liquids a little) and check the result.
• If you're baking a large loaf (more than 450g/1lb), let it rest longer, and let it bake longer by 10 to 15 minutes.

One final word of advice: if you're finding the breads just a little gummy, don't slice or eat your loaves when they're still warm. We know, hot bread has a certain romance, so it's hard to wait for it to cool. But waiting will improve the texture, and when cool, the loaves don't compress so easily when cut. A sharp bread knife will go right through cooled crust and crumb with minimal compression.

Top crust won't crisp and brown nicely:
- Be sure you're using a baking stone where called for, and preheat it for at least 30 minutes, in an oven whose temperature has been checked with a thermometer.
- Bake with steam when called for, and be sure to close the oven door quickly after pouring hot water onto the grill tray to trap steam, which is key to creating a crackling crust.

If you're a crisp crust fanatic, we'll give you one ultimate approach to baking the perfect crust, but it takes some extra work (this does not apply to enriched breads). Start the loaf on the bottom shelf, directly on the stone. Two-thirds of the way through baking, transfer the loaf from the stone on the bottom shelf directly to a rack on the top shelf of the oven, removing the water pan (leave the stone where it is). Top crusts brown best near the top of the oven, and bottom crusts brown best near the bottom. This approach is particularly helpful with hard-crusted loaf-tin breads, where popping the bread out of the pan and transferring shelves makes a big difference in the crispness of the side and bottom crusts.

With this approach, you can permanently park your baking stone on the very lowest rack, where it will help even out the heat for everything you bake, not just bread. Then there'll be no need to shift around the stone or racks just because you're baking bread.

Overbaking Problems

The crust is great, but the crumb (interior) is dry:

• The bread may be overbaked. Again, make sure your oven is calibrated properly, using an oven thermometer.

• Another possibility is that the dough was dry to begin with. In traditional recipes, there's usually an instruction that reads something like 'knead thoroughly, until the mass of dough is smooth, elastic and less sticky, adding flour as needed'. This often means too much flour gets added. Be careful not to add much additional flour when shaping.

Flour blobs in the middle of the slices: These are usually related to having added too much flour. Using wet hands to incorporate the last bits of flour will take care of this problem.

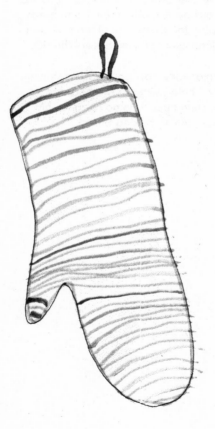

Shaping Problems

Loaf flattens and spreads sideways while resting on the pizza peel: If every loaf is ending up as flat bread, there are several possible explanations . . .

- The dough is too wet. This is often the problem when mixing by hand and there's an incentive to cut off the flour too soon (it's easier on your wrists).
- Not enough flour was dusted onto the dough while shaping and cloaking the loaf.
- The dough is too old. At about the point where it becomes 'weepy', with liquid separating out from the dough, it's probably lost too much rising power to produce beautiful, domed loaves. It will still taste good, but it will turn into flat bread every time, unless you bake it in a loaf tin.

Odd-shaped loaves: If you haven't used enough polenta or flour on the pizza peel, a spot of dough may stick to it. As you slide the loaf off the peel, the spot pulls, causing an odd-shaped loaf. Solution: use more polenta or flour on the pizza peel, especially if the dough is particularly sticky. You may also add flour to the dough during the cloaking and shaping step.

Other causes of odd-shaped loaves include not slashing deeply enough, and not letting the shaped loaves rest long enough before baking.

Extending the rest time after shaping: Throughout the book, we specify a short rest after shaping, and for most people this will work well. Others, who may prefer lighter bread, or wholemeal flours, or who are resting the loaves in a cool environment (less than 19°C), may find that they prefer a longer rest. The range for the rest time is 40 to 90 minutes, tending toward the longer end of that when it's cool or if there's whole grain in the loaf. This is a matter of taste, so experiment. Loosely cover the resting loaf with plastic wrap if you're resting the loaf for longer than 60 minutes.

Storing Bread

Bread is at its best when it has completely cooled after baking. Hot or warm bread has a romantic appeal, but it cuts poorly and dries out quickly. And that certainly doesn't make for good storing characteristics. Having said that, sometimes we just can't resist!

We've found that the best way to keep bread fresh once it has been cut is to store it cut side down on a flat, non-porous surface like a plate or a clean worktop. Don't use foil, clingfilm or bags, which trap humidity. This softens the crust by allowing it to absorb water. An exception is pitta bread, which is supposed to have a soft crust and can be stored in a plastic bag once cooled.

Breads made with whole grains or lots of water, and breads made with dough that has been well aged stay fresh longest. Keep that in mind if you would prefer to bake every other day. Use day-old bread for making bread crumbs in the food processor, or try one of our recipes like *panzanella* (page 68), bread puddings (pages 246 and 248), or *fattoush* (page 181). Or recycle your stale bread into new loaves as *altus* (page 90).

Par-baking Artisan Breads

Par-baking means partially baking your loaves, with the intention of finishing the baking later. In our attempt to improve the quality of our lives and the food we eat while reducing the time spent doing just that, we decided to test the concept of par-baking. Par-baking allows you to do all the shaping and most of the baking at home, and then complete it later. The par-baked bread can even be frozen. The perfect opportunity for this approach is when you're invited to a friend's house for dinner. Complete the baking in their oven and you present an absolutely fresh and warm bread for the dinner party.

Baking instructions for par-baked bread:
1. Follow preparation steps for any recipe in this book.
2. Begin baking at the recipe's usual temperature.
3. Remove the loaf from the oven when it just begins to darken in colour; the idea is to set the centre of the loaf. For most loaves, that means about 90 per cent of the baking time.
4. Allow the loaf to cool on a rack, and then place in a plastic bag. Freeze immediately if you plan on storing bread for more than a day. If you don't have time to let the loaf cool, transport it in a brown paper bag to allow moisture to escape or the bread may become soggy.

To complete the baking:
1. If frozen, completely defrost the loaf at room temperature. Place on a baking stone in an oven preheated to the recipe's recommended temperature. Bake until browned and appealing, usually about 5 to 10 minutes.
2. Cool on a rack as usual.

THE MASTER RECIPE

We chose the artisan free-form loaf called the French boule as the basic model for all the breads in this book. The dough is made with white flour, yeast, salt and water; it is the easiest to handle and most reliable to bake successfully. The white dough is used to make all the recipes in this chapter; later chapters and recipes introduce other flours and flavours. The round free-form shape of the boule ('boule' in French means 'ball') is the easiest to master. You'll learn how wet the dough needs to be (wet, but not so wet that the finished loaf won't hold its shape) and how a 'gluten cloak' substitutes for kneading. And you'll learn a truly revolutionary approach to bread baking: take the needed amount of pre-mixed dough from the fridge, shape it, leave it to rest, then pop it in the oven and let it bake while you're preparing the rest of the meal.

Keep your dough wet – wetter doughs create an environment that favours the development of sourdough character over the week of storage. And by omitting kneading, by mixing dough in bulk, then storing and using it as it's needed over time, you'll truly be able to make this bread in 5 minutes a day (excluding resting and oven time). **You should become familiar with the following recipe before going through the rest of the book.**

The Master Recipe:
Boule (Artisan Free-Form Loaf)

Makes four 450g/1lb loaves. The recipe is easily doubled or halved.

- 750ml/1¼ pints lukewarm water
- 1½ tbsp granulated yeast
  (decrease according to taste, see page 23)
- 1½ tbsp coarse grain salt
  (decrease according to taste, see page 25)
- 900g/2lb unsifted,
  unbleached, plain white flour
- Polenta or parchment paper for pizza peel,
  see page 29

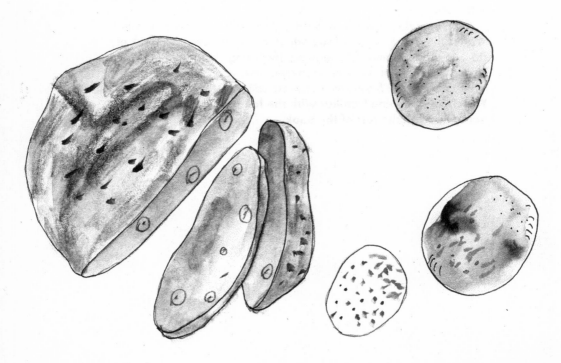

Mixing and Storing the Dough

1. **Warm the water slightly:** It should feel just a little warmer than body temperature, about 38°C. Warm water will rise the dough to the right point for storage in about 2 hours. You can use cold tap water and get an identical final result; then the first rising will take 3 or even 4 hours. That won't be too great a difference, as you will only be doing this once per stored batch.

2. **Add yeast and salt to the water** in a 5 litre/8¾ pint bowl or, preferably, in a resealable, lidded (not airtight) plastic food container or bucket. Don't worry about getting it all to dissolve.

3. **Mix in the flour – kneading is unnecessary:** Add all of the flour at once, mix with a wooden spoon, a high-capacity food processor (3.5 litres/6 pints or larger) fitted with the dough attachment, or a heavy-duty stand mixer fitted with the dough hook until the mixture is uniform. If you're hand-mixing and it becomes too difficult to incorporate all the flour with the spoon, you can reach into your mixing vessel with very wet hands and press the mixture together. Don't knead! It isn't necessary. You're finished when everything is uniformly moist, without dry patches. This step is done in a matter of minutes, and will yield a dough that is wet and loose enough to conform to the shape of its container.

4. **Allow to rise:** Cover with a lid (not airtight) that fits well to the container you're using. Allow the mixture to rise at room temperature until it begins to collapse (or at least flattens on the top), approximately 2 hours, depending on the room's temperature and the initial water temperature. Longer rising times, up to about 5 hours, will not harm the result. You can use a portion of the dough any time after this period. Fully refrigerated wet dough is less sticky and is easier to work with than dough at room temperature. So, the first time you try our method, it's best to refrigerate the dough overnight (or at least 3 hours), before shaping a loaf.

Relax! You do not need to monitor doubling or tripling of volume as in traditional recipes.

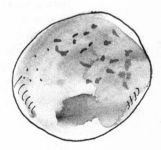

What's a 'gluten cloak'?

Just imagine a warm blanket being pulled around you on a cold night. Or, for the more technically inclined, what you are trying to do here is to add enough flour to the surface so it can be handled and the protein strands in the surface can be aligned, creating a resilient 'cloak' around the mass of wet, barely kneaded dough. Visualise a cloak being pulled around the dough, so that the entire ball is surrounded by a skin. Resist the temptation to get rid of all stickiness by adding too much flour. Adding large amounts of flour prevents the bread from achieving a finished crumb with the typical artisanal 'custard' (page 33).

Steam alternatives

Some oven doors (and most professional ones) don't make a great seal for holding in steam. If your oven allows steam to dissipate and you're not getting a beautiful crust, try one of these two alternatives to the grill tray method:

Food-grade water sprayer: Mist the bread three times with water from the spray during the first two minutes of baking.

Metal bowl or aluminum-foiling roasting pan for covering loaves in the oven: By trapping steam next to a loaf as it bakes on the hot stone, you can create the humid environment that produces a crisp crust without using a grill tray or a sprayer. The bowl or dish needs to be heat-tolerant and tall enough so that the rising loaf won't touch it when it rises, but not so large that it hangs beyond the edge of the stone, or it won't trap the steam. This is a great technique for outdoor grills, which don't trap steam even when the lid is down.

On Baking Day

5. **The gluten cloak:** Don't knead, just 'cloak' and shape a loaf in 30 to 60 seconds. First, prepare a pizza peel by sprinkling it liberally with polenta (or whatever your recipe calls for) to prevent your loaf from sticking to it when you slide it into the oven.

   Sprinkle the surface of your refrigerated dough with flour. Pull up and cut off a 450g/ 1lb (grapefruit-size) piece of dough, using a serrated knife. Hold the mass of dough in your hands and add a little more flour as needed so it won't stick to your hands. Gently stretch the surface of the dough around to the bottom on all four sides, rotating the ball a quarter turn as you go. Most of the dusting flour will fall off; it's not intended to be incorporated into the dough. The bottom of the loaf may appear to be a collection of bunched ends, but it will flatten out and adhere during resting and baking. The correctly shaped final product will be smooth and cohesive. The entire process should take no more than 20 to 40 seconds.

6. **Rest the loaf and let it rise on a pizza peel:** Place the shaped ball on the polenta-covered pizza peel (see p. 28 under Pizza Peel for alternatives). Allow the loaf to rest on the peel for about 40 minutes (consider a longer rest time if you're finding your results to be denser than you like, see page 39). It doesn't need to be covered during the rest period. Depending on the age of the dough, you may not see much rise during this period; more rising will occur during baking ('oven spring').

7. **Thirty minutes before baking, preheat the oven to 230°C/gas mark 8,** with a baking stone placed on the middle rack. Place an empty grill tray for holding water on any other shelf that won't interfere with the rising bread.

8. **Dust and slash:** Unless otherwise indicated in a specific recipe, dust the top of the loaf liberally with flour, which will allow the slashing knife to pass without sticking. Slash a 5mm/ ¼in-deep cross, scallop or criss-cross pattern into the top, using a serrated bread knife.

9. **Baking with steam:** After a 30-minute preheat, you're ready to bake. With a quick forward jerking motion of the wrist, slide the loaf off the pizza peel and onto the preheated baking stone. Quickly but carefully pour about 250ml/8 fl oz of hot water from the tap into the grill tray and close the oven door to trap the steam. Bake for about 30 minutes, or until the crust is nicely browned and firm; there is little risk of drying out the interior, despite the dark crust. When you remove the loaf from the oven, it will audibly crackle, or 'sing', when initially exposed to room-temperature air. Allow to cool completely, preferably on a wire cooling rack, for best flavour, texture and slicing. The perfect crust may initially soften, but will firm up again when cooled.

10. Store the remaining dough in the fridge in your lidded (not airtight) container and use it over the next 14 days: You'll find that even one day's storage improves the flavour and texture of your bread. This maturation continues over the 14-day storage period. Refrigerate unused dough in a lidded storage container (again, not airtight – just crack the lid a little, or punch a small hole in the plastic lid). If you mixed your dough in this container, you've avoided some washing up. Cut off and shape more loaves as you need them. We often have several types of dough storing in the fridge at once. The dough can also be frozen in 450g/1lb portions in an airtight container and defrosted overnight in the fridge prior to baking day.

Lazy sourdough shortcut: When your dough bucket is finally empty, don't wash it! Immediately re-mix another batch in the same container. In addition to saving the washing-up step, the aged dough stuck to the sides of the container will give your new batch a head start on sourdough flavour. Just scrape it down and it will hydrate and incorporate into the new dough.

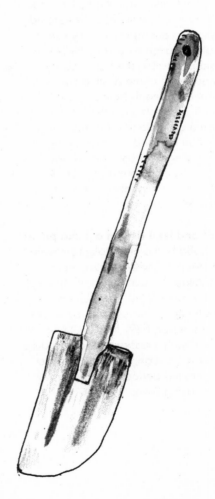

Variation: Herb Bread

This simple recipe shows off the versatility of our approach. Herb-scented breads are great favourites for appetisers and snacks.

Follow the directions for mixing the Boule dough and add 1 teaspoon dried thyme leaves (2 teaspoons fresh) and ½ teaspoon dried rosemary leaves (1 teaspoon fresh) to the water mixture.

You can also use herbs with the other bread recipes in this chapter.

Baguette

This is the quintessential thin and crusty loaf of France, served at every meal, and the symbol of their entire cuisine. We both travelled there with our spouses, years apart, and had the same response to the mood, to the light, to the sounds, and maybe most of all, to the flavours, especially the baguettes.

A 20-minute rest after shaping is all that is needed to create a light and airy loaf. So our baguette is delicious, and very, very fast.

Baguettes are defined as much by their crust as their crumb (the bread's interior). The crust dominates the mouth sensation. Aside from the shape, one important technique that differentiates the baguette from the boule in this chapter is that the baguette is not heavily dusted with flour, at least not traditionally. So, to keep the knife from sticking, brush water onto the surface of the loaf just before slashing. You'll also notice that this loaf uses wholemeal flour rather than polenta on the pizza peel, since polenta would impart too strong a flavour for classic baguettes. Traditional recipes for baguettes are high maintenance, so if you've done this the old-fashioned way, our approach should be a relief. With your fresh baguette, create a sensational meal by making an Aubergine Tartine (page 52).

Makes 1 large or 2 small baguettes.

• 450g/1lb (grapefruit-size portion) Boule dough (page 44)
• Wholemeal flour or parchment paper for pizza peel, see page 29

1. Thirty minutes before baking time, Preheat the oven to 230°C/gas mark 8 with a baking stone placed on the middle rack. Place an empty grill tray on any other shelf that won't interfere with the rising bread.

2. Dust the surface of the refrigerated dough with flour and cut off a 450g/1lb (grapefruit-size) piece. Dust the piece with more flour and shape it into a ball by stretching the surface of the dough around to the bottom on all four sides, rotating the ball a quarter turn as you go. Once it's cohesive, begin to stretch and elongate the dough, dusting with additional flour as necessary. You may find it helpful to roll it back and forth with your hands on a floured surface. Form a cylinder approximately 5cm/2in in diameter. If the loaf won't fit on your pizza peel or stone, cut it in half to make two smaller baguettes. Place the loaf/loaves on a pizza peel covered with wholemeal flour and allow to rest for 20 minutes.

3. After the dough has rested, paint water over the surface of the loaf using a pastry brush. The water prevents the knife from sticking in the wet dough, and an authentic baguette isn't flourdusted on the top crust. Slash the loaf with longitudinal cuts that move diagonally across the loaf, using a serrated bread knife.

4. Slide the loaf directly onto the hot stone. Pour 250ml/8 fl oz of hot tap water into the grill tray, and quickly close the oven door. Bake for about 25 minutes, or until deeply browned and firm to the touch.

5. Allow to cool on a rack before cutting or eating.

Aubergine Tartine

This open sandwich is a more sophisticated and vegetarian cousin to our Croque Monsieur (page 220), with smoky grilled aubergine and red pepper on freshly baked Baguette (page 50), topped with peppery greens and soft, ripe cheese.

Makes 1 open baguette sandwich to serve 3 or 4.

- 2 x 1cm/½in-thick pieces of lengthwise-sliced aubergine
- Olive oil for brushing aubergine
- Salt and pepper to taste
- ½ red pepper
- ½ baguette (see page 50)
- 2 cloves roasted garlic (see page 137, step 1)
- 1 dozen rocket leaves
- 75g/3oz soft ripened cheese such as Brie or Camembert, sliced

1. Preheat a gas or charcoal barbecue, or a grill. Brush the aubergine slices with olive oil. Sprinkle with salt and pepper and cook over a medium gas flame or charcoal, or under a grill, until browned and soft but not overcooked, approximately 5 minutes on each side.

2. Cut the halved pepper in two again and then flatten the pieces, making additional cuts as needed to flatten. Cook the pepper under the grill or on the gas or charcoal barbecue, keeping the skin side closer to the heat source. Check often and remove when the skin is blackened, about 8 to 10 minutes. Drop the roasted pieces into an empty bowl and cover it. The skin will loosen over the next ten minutes. Gently peel the pepper by hand and discard the blackened skin. Some dark bits will adhere to the pepper flesh, which won't be a problem. Cut the pepper into thin ribbons.

3. Split the baguette lengthwise, spread it open, and tear out some of the inside. Smear roasted garlic over the cut surface. Top with aubergine and sliced pepper. Spread rocket over the pepper.

4. Top with the cheese and grill for 3 to 4 minutes, until the cheese is melted, taking care not to burn the baguettes.

Bâtard

This short and wide baguette-style loaf is easier to use for sandwiches because there's more of the chewy interior compared to the crustier baguette. Accordingly, the flavour leans towards the mellow sweetness of the crumb rather than the crisp caramelisation of the crust. Depending on your preference, this loaf can be almost as wide as a sandwich loaf, but typically it is about 7.5cm/3in across at its widest point. Like baguettes, the bâtard is tapered to a point at each end.

Makes 1 bâtard.

- 450g/1lb (grapefruit-size portion) Boule dough (page 44)
- Wholemeal flour or parchment paper for pizza peel, see page 29

1. Follow steps 1 and 2 for the baguette on page 51, but shape the loaf to a diameter of about 7.5cm/3in.

2. When rolling the loaf on the floured surface, concentrate pressure at the ends to form the bâtard's traditional taper.

3. Follow steps 3 to 5 for the baguette, but increase the baking time to 30 minutes, or until deeply brown.

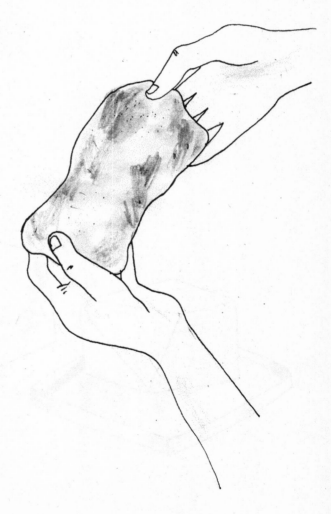

Couronne

This ring or crown-shaped French loaf is a speciality of Lyon. It's quite simple to shape and is a beautiful, crustier alternative to the classic boule.

Makes 1 couronne.

- 450g/1lb (grapefruit-size portion) Boule dough (page 44)
- Wholemeal flour or parchment paper for pizza peel, see page 29

1. Dust the surface of the refrigerated dough with flour and cut off a 450g/1lb (grapefruit-size) piece. Dust the piece with more flour and quickly shape it into a ball by stretching the surface of the dough around to the bottom on all four sides, rotating the ball a quarter turn as you go. When a cohesive ball has formed, poke your thumbs through the centre of the ball and gradually stretch the hole so that it will be large enough to stay open during the oven rise of the bread. This means that the hole will need to be about three times as wide as the wall of the ring.

2. Place the loaf on a pizza peel covered with wholemeal flour and allow to rest for 40 minutes (consider a longer rest time if you're finding your results to be denser than you like, see page 39).

3. Thirty minutes before baking time, preheat the oven to 230°C/gas mark 8, with a baking stone placed on the middle rack (consider a longer preheat if you're finding your results to be denser than you like, see page 34). Place an empty grill tray on any other shelf that won't interfere with the rising bread.

4. Just before baking, dust the couronne with flour and slash radially, like spokes in a wheel.

5. Slide the loaf directly onto the hot stone. Pour 250ml/8 fl oz of hot tap water into the grill tray, and quickly close the oven door. Bake for about 30 minutes, or until deeply browned and firm. Smaller or larger loaves will require adjustments in baking time.

6. Allow the bread to cool before cutting or eating.

Ciabatta

The word *ciabatta* is Italian for slipper, and refers to the shape of the bread, which is halfway between a flatbread and a loaf-shaped bread. It's made from very wet dough, shaped as a elongated oval or rectangle (perhaps you have slippers shaped like this?). To achieve the very moist crumb, shape the loaf with wet hands, rather than dusting with flour. The bread will be chewy and moist, with large and appealing air holes. Ciabatta is baked without polenta on the bottom, so dust the pizza peel with a thick coating of white flour instead. And, since white flour is a less efficient 'stick-preventer' than polenta, you may need to nudge the loaf off the peel with a metal dough scraper or spatula.

Makes 1 ciabatta.

• 450g/1lb (grapefruit-size portion) Boule dough (page 44)
• White flour for the pizza peel

1. Cut off a 450g/1lb (grapefruit-size) piece of refrigerated dough without dusting the surface with flour; wet hands will help prevent sticking. Using your wet hands, shape the dough into a ball by stretching the surface of the dough around to the bottom on all four sides, rotating the ball a quarter turn as you go. With your wet fingers, flatten the ball into an elongated oval about 2cm/¾in thick. Don't make it thinner than 2cm/¾in, or it will puff like pitta bread, which isn't desirable here.

2. Thirty minutes before baking time, preheat the oven to 230°C/gas mark 8, with a baking stone placed on the middle rack (consider a longer preheat if you're finding your results to be denser than you like, see page 34). Place an empty grill tray on any other shelf that won't interfere with the rising bread.

3. Place the loaf on a flour-covered pizza peel and allow to rest for 20 minutes. Dust the top with flour, but don't slash the loaf.

4. Slide the loaf directly onto the hot stone. Pour 250ml/8 fl oz of hot tap water into the grill tray, and quickly close the oven door. Bake for about 20 minutes, or until deeply brown.

5. Allow to cool on a rack before cutting or eating.

Pain d'Epí
(Wheat Stalk Bread)

This is a simple yet impressive bread to present to guests. You may find that you get more well-defined 'wheat grains' when you use high-protein strong flour as listed below. However you can use plain flour, but increase it to 980g/1lb 3oz. The bread can also be made with our master white dough (see Boule, page 44), but the illusion of the wheat grains won't be quite so well-defined.

'I first ate pain d'epí when vacationing in the south of France. Maman, our adopted grandmother and host, had it delivered fresh every morning. I'd walk through a yard filled with fruit and herb trees to a special bread basket that hung next to the postbox. I'd pick up this freshly baked wheat stalk and have to pinch myself to make sure it wasn't a dream. The bread was impossibly light, crisp, and absolutely perfect with coffee and jam in the morning, or with Maman's fish stew for dinner. It was heaven!' – Zoë

Makes four 450g/1lb loaves. The recipe is easily doubled or halved.

- 750ml/1¼ pints lukewarm water
- 1½ tbsp granulated yeast (decrease according to taste, see page 23)
- 1½ tbsp coarse grain salt (decrease according to taste, see page 25)
- 900g/2lb strong flour
- Parchment paper for the pizza peel

1. Mixing and storing the dough: mix the yeast and salt with the water.

2. Mix in the flour without kneading, using a spoon, a 3.5 litre/6 pint-capacity food processor (with dough attachment), or a heavy-duty stand mixer (with dough hook). If you're not using a machine, you may need to use wet hands to get the last bit of flour to incorporate.

3. Cover (not airtight), and allow to rest at room temperature until the dough rises and collapses (or flattens on top); approximately 2 hours.

4. The dough can be used immediately after the initial rise, though it is easier to handle when cold. Refrigerate in a lidded (not airtight) container and use over the next 14 days.

5. On baking day, dust the surface of the refrigerated dough with flour and cut off a 450g/1lb (grapefruit-size) piece. Dust the piece with more flour and quickly shape it into a ball by stretching the surface of the dough around to the bottom on all four sides, rotating the ball a quarter turn as you go. Gradually elongate the mass. With the palms of your hands, gently roll it into the shape of a baguette, tapering the ends to points.

6. Allow to rest and rise on a parchment paper-covered pizza peel for 30 minutes. Do not slash.

7. Thirty minutes before baking time, preheat the oven to 230°C/gas mark 8, with a baking stone placed on the middle rack (consider a longer preheat if you're finding your results to be denser than you like, see page 34). Place an empty grill tray on any other shelf that won't interfere with the rising bread. Just before baking time, dust the loaf with flour. With a sharp pair of kitchen scissors, cut from the top, at an angle of 45° into the dough, stopping 5mm/¼in from the bottom. Fold each cut piece over to the side, alternating sides with each cut. Repeat until the entire loaf is cut and pain d'epí formed.

8. Slide the loaf directly onto the hot stone. Pour 250ml/8 fl oz of hot tap water into the grill tray, and quickly close the oven door. Bake for about 25 minutes, or until the loaf is deeply browned and firm.

9. Allow to cool before breaking off the wheat-stalk shapes. Slather with butter and eat warm if you can't wait!

Crusty White Sandwich Loaf

This loaf is nothing like commercial white bread, that impossibly soft stuff best used for wadding up and tossing across lunchrooms. The crust is firm if not actually crackling. If you're looking for a flavourful, soft-crusted and buttery loaf, closer to what most kids are used to, you'll probably want to try Soft American-Style White Bread (page 218) or Buttermilk Bread (page 222). The stored dough adds sourdough complexity to the traditionally bland product, and the steam adds both crackle and caramelisation to the crust.

This variation will give you some experience baking high-moisture dough in a loaf tin. You must use a non-stick tin; they work well but still require a light greasing. Wet dough usually sticks miserably to traditional pans no matter how much you grease them.

Makes 1 loaf.

- 675g/1½lb (cantaloupe melon-size portion) Boule dough (page 44)
- Neutral-tasting oil for greasing the tin

1. Dust the surface of the refrigerated dough with flour and cut off a 675g/1½lb (cantaloupe melon-size) piece. Dust with more flour and quickly shape it into a ball by stretching the surface of the dough around to the bottom on all four sides, rotating the ball a quarter turn as you go. Lightly grease a 23 x 10 x 7.5cm/ 9 x 4 x 3in non-stick loaf tin with a neutral-flavoured oil.

2. Elongate the ball into an oval and drop it into the prepared tin. You want to fill the tin slightly more than half full.

3. Allow the dough to rest for 1 hour and 40 minutes; (or just 40 minutes if you're using fresh, unrefrigerated dough). Dust with flour and slash the top crust with the tip of a serrated bread knife.

4. Thirty minutes before baking time, preheat the oven to 230°C/gas mark 8, with an empty grill tray on any other shelf that won't interfere with the rising bread. A baking stone is not essential when using a loaf tin; if you omit it, you can shorten the preheating time to 5 minutes.

5. Place the loaf on a rack near the centre of the oven. Pour 250ml/8 fl oz of hot tap water into the grill tray and quickly close the oven door. Bake for about 35 minutes, or until brown and firm.

6. Remove the loaf from the pan and allow to cool completely on a rack before slicing or eating.

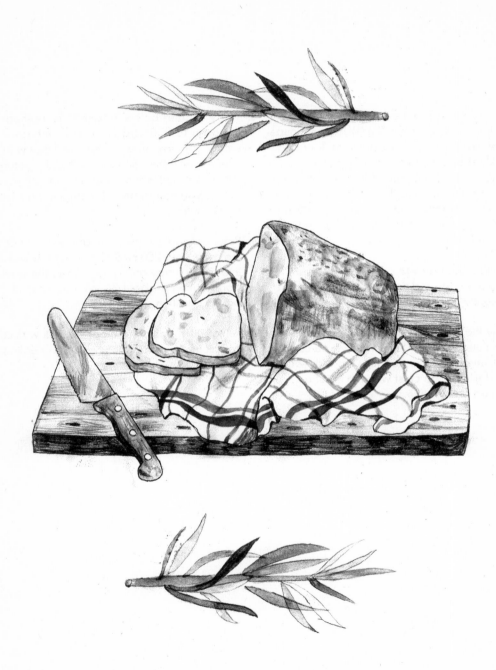

PEASANT LOAVES

The term 'peasant bread' has come to mean the rougher, more rustic loaf that originated in the European countryside during the Middle Ages. These are breads made with whole-grain ingredients that, once upon a time, fell out of fashion with sophisticated European urbanites. How times have changed; since the 1980s, rustic breads now signal sophistication just as surely as a perfect French baguette. Forget sophistication; thank goodness we've come to realise the wonderful and complex flavours to be had by adding whole grains and rye to our bread.

Rye flour creates the tangy, slightly nutty fragrance and flavour that is basic to many of these breads, whether or not it's blended with wholemeal or other grains. Even if rye flour is not sold as 'whole grain', it has more fibre (from rye bran) than white wheat flour. The proteins and starches in rye flour plus the extra boost of rye bran mean that the breads have a substantial texture and sensation when chewed.

European Peasant Bread

The round, whole-grain country-style loaves of rural France (*pain de campagne*) and Italy (*pane rustico*) were the natural results of European poverty where white flour was once an almost unattainable luxury. Today people from all walks of life enjoy the crackling crust and moist chewy crumb that are the key sensations of this peasant bread.

We live in the upper Midwest region of America, where in the wintertime we dream of vacations along the sunny Riviera. The next best thing to being there is mixing up a batch of this bread and serving it with anchovies, a strong cheese and a hearty fish soup with lots of garlic and fresh herbs (see page 104). We are utterly transported!

Next day, cut up the leftovers for Tuscan Bread Salad (page 68).

Makes four 450g/1lb loaves. The recipe is easily doubled or halved.

- 750ml/1¼ pints lukewarm water
- 1½ tbsp granulated yeast (decrease according to taste, see page 23)
- 1½ tbsp coarse grain salt (decrease according to taste, see page 25)
- 70g/2½oz rye flour
- 70g/2½oz wholemeal flour
- 770g/1lb 11oz unbleached plain flour
- Polenta or parchment paper for pizza peel, see page 29

1. Mixing and storing the dough: mix the yeast and salt with the water in a 5 litre/8¾ pint bowl, or a lidded (not airtight) food container.

2. Mix in the remaining dry ingredients without kneading, using a spoon, a 3.5 litre/6 pint-capacity food processor (with dough attachment), or a heavy-duty stand mixer (with dough hook). If you're not using a machine, you may need to use wet hands to incorporate the last bit of flour.

3. Cover (not airtight), and allow to rest at room temperature until the dough rises and collapses (or flattens on top), approximately 2 hours.

4. The dough can be used immediately after the initial rise, though it is easier to handle when cold. Refrigerate in a lidded (not airtight) container and use over the next 14 days.

5. On baking day, dust the surface of the refrigerated dough with flour and cut off a 450g/1lb (grapefruit-size) piece. Dust with more flour and quickly shape it into a ball by stretching the surface of the dough around to the bottom on all four sides, rotating the ball a quarter turn as you go. Allow to rest and rise on a polenta-covered pizza peel for 40 minutes (consider a longer rest time if you're finding your results to be denser than you like, see page 39).

6. Thirty minutes before baking time, preheat the oven to 230°C/gas mark 8, with a baking stone placed on the middle rack (consider a longer preheat if you're finding your results to be denser than you like, see page 34). Place an empty grill tray on any other shelf that won't interfere with the rising bread.

7. Sprinkle the loaf liberally with flour and slash a deep cross, scallop, or criss-cross pattern into the top, using a serrated bread knife. Leave the flour in place for baking; tap some of it off before slicing.

8. Slide the loaf directly onto the hot stone. Pour 250ml/8 fl oz of hot tap water into the grill tray, and quickly close the oven door. Bake for about 35 minutes, or until the top crust is deeply browned and very firm. Smaller or larger loaves will require adjustments in baking time.

9. Allow to cool before slicing or eating.

Tuscan Bread Salad (Panzanella)

Even great bread goes stale; here's a delicious way to use it. European Peasant Bread is our first choice for Panzanella, but most other non-enriched, unsweetened breads will also work well. This salad is a masterpiece when made with tomatoes at the peak of the summer season. If you grow your own, here's your chance to let them shine. If you want to turn this into a complete vegetarian meal, add cooked or canned cannellini beans.

Makes 4 servings.

The Salad
- 10 slices stale bread (1 to 3 days old), cubed
- 3 medium tomatoes, cubed
- 1 medium cucumber, sliced
- 1 very small red onion, thinly sliced
- 1 tsp capers
- 25g/1oz pitted black olives, halved
- 2 anchovy fillets, chopped, optional
- 15 basil leaves, coarsely chopped
- 1 tbsp coarsely grated Parmigiano Reggiano cheese
- 75g/3oz cooked or canned cannellini or beans (optional)

The Dressing
- 75ml/2½ fl oz extra virgin olive oil
- 3 tsp red wine vinegar
- 1 garlic clove, finely chopped
- Salt and freshly ground pepper to taste (don't be stingy)

1. Prepare the salad ingredients and combine in a large salad bowl.

2. Whisk all the dressing ingredients until well blended.

3. Toss the dressing with the salad, and allow to stand for at least 10 minutes, or until the bread has softened.

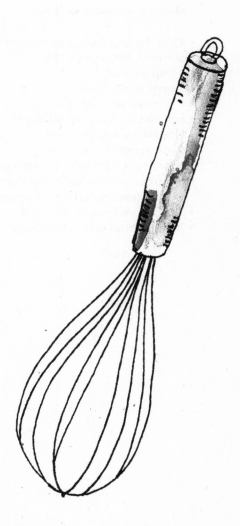

Pan Bagna (Provençal Tuna and Vegetable Sandwich)

This sandwich loaf is a speciality of Provence, where generations of farm families came up with ways to use day-old country bread. *Pan bagna*, literally translated from the Provençal language, means 'bathed bread'. You'll have an easier time with this recipe if you shape a slightly flattened boule, rather than a high-domed one.

Makes 4 sandwich wedges.

- 450g/1lb loaf European Peasant Bread (page 66), or French Boule (page 44)
- 4 tbsp olive oil
- 1 small garlic clove
- 1 tbsp red wine vinegar
- Salt and freshly ground pepper
- 115g/4oz soft goat's cheese
- 6 olives, pitted and sliced
- 40g/1½oz rocket leaves, rinsed and well dried
- 175g/6oz cooked fresh tuna steak, thinly sliced, or substitute canned tuna if you can't get fresh
- 3 small tomatoes, thinly sliced
- 10 large basil leaves, shredded

1. Slice the bread in half horizontally and slightly hollow out the top and the bottom. Make fresh bread crumbs out of the discarded centres and keep for another use. Drizzle the cut surface of the halves with 1½ tablespoons of the oil.

2. In a blender combine the remaining 2½ tablespoons of oil with the garlic, vinegar and salt to taste. Blend the dressing until smooth.

3. Spread the goat's cheese in the bottom shell and top it with the olives, rocket and salt and pepper to taste. Drizzle with one third of the dressing, top with the tuna, salt and pepper to taste, and drizzle half the remaining dressing over the tuna. Top the tuna with the tomatoes, basil and salt and pepper to taste. Drizzle with the remaining dressing, and add the top of the loaf.

4. Wrap the sandwich in clingfilm, place it on a plate, and cover it with another plate with approximately 450–900g/1–2lb of weight on top. Refrigerate for 1 hour, or eat right away if you can't wait. The sandwich may be made up to 6 hours in advance and kept covered and chilled.

5. Allow to come partway back to room temperature, cut the *pan bagna* into 5cm/2in slices, and serve.

Olive Bread

This bread is associated with the countries of the Mediterranean, especially Italy and France, where the olives are abundant and have incredible flavour. Use the best-quality olives you can find; the wetter Kalamata style work as well as the dry Niçoise type, so it's your choice. The rich salty flavours of the olives make this a perfect accompaniment to cheeses, pasta tossed with fresh tomatoes or our Tuscan White Bean Dip (page 74).

Makes 1 olive bread.

Use any of these pre-mixed doughs: Boule (page 44), European Peasant (page 66), Olive Oil (page 150), Light Wholemeal (page 94) or Italian Semolina (page 100).

• 450g/1lb (grapefruit-size portion) of any pre-mixed dough listed above
• 25g/1oz high-quality olives, pitted and halved
• Cornflour wash (see box)
• Polenta or parchment paper for pizza peel, see page 29

1. Dust the surface of the refrigerated dough with flour and cut off a grapefruit-size piece. Using your hands and a rolling pin, flatten the dough to a thickness of 1cm/½in. Cover with the olives and roll up to seal inside the dough. Dust with more flour and quickly shape it into a ball by stretching the surface of the dough around to the bottom on all four sides, rotating the ball a quarter turn as you go. Allow to rest and rise on a polenta-covered pizza peel for 1 hour.

2. Thirty minutes before baking time, preheat the oven to 230°C/gas mark 8, with a baking stone placed on the middle rack (consider a longer preheat if you're finding your results to be denser than you like, see page 34). Place an empty grill tray on any other shelf that won't interfere with the rising bread.

3. Just before baking, paint the surface of the loaf with cornflour wash, then slash a deep cross, scallop or criss-cross pattern into the top, using a serrated bread knife.

4. Slide the loaf directly onto the hot stone. Pour 250ml/8 fl oz of hot tap water into the grill tray, and quickly close the oven door. Bake for about 35 minutes, or until the top crust is deeply browned and very firm.

5. Allow to cool on a rack before slicing or eating.

Cornflour Wash

Using a fork, blend ½ teaspoon cornflour with a small amount of water to form a paste. Add 120ml/4 fl oz water and whisk with the fork. Microwave or boil until mixture appears glassy, about 30 to 60 seconds on high. It will keep in the fridge for two weeks; discard if it has an off smell.

Tuscan White Bean Dip

All across Europe, meals are made up of beans mixed with other savoury flavours such as garlic and basil and served with a variety of meats. We created this dip in the spirit of simplifying our lives and eating foods with rich, wonderful flavours. Simply purée beans with the aromatics and spread it over our Olive Bread (page 72) to make this delicious rustic hors d'oeuvre.

And if you don't have time to roast the garlic, raw is fine, though it will have a much stronger kick. Canned roasted red peppers can be substituted, but the flavour is less intense.

Makes about 450g/1lb of dip.

- 175g/6oz dried cannellini beans (or 450g can cannellini beans, drained)
- 1 small red pepper
- 1 large clove roasted garlic (page 137, step 1)
- 2 tbsp extra virgin olive oil
- 1 tsp salt (decrease according to taste, see page 25)
- Freshly ground pepper to taste
- 10 fresh basil leaves

1. Pick over the dried beans for stones, dirt and debris. Rinse, drain and then cover with water and soak overnight. Bring to a simmer and cook for 2 to 3 hours, or until soft, adding water as needed to keep the beans covered. Drain, reserving about 475ml/16 fl oz of the cooking liquid (though you probably won't need all of it). If using canned beans, discard the canning liquid and use plain water later in the recipe.

2. Cut the pepper into quarters, remove the core and seeds, and then flatten the pieces, cutting additional slits as needed. Grill or barbecue the pepper under the grill or on a gas or charcoal barbecue until the skin is blackened, about 8 to 10 minutes. Drop the roasted pepper into a tightly covered bowl and allow the skin to loosen by 'steaming' in its own heat and moisture for 10 minutes or longer. Gently peel the pepper by hand and discard the blackened skin. Some dark bits will adhere to the pepper flesh.

3. Peel the roasted garlic and place it in the food processor along with the cooked beans, olive oil, salt and pepper. Process until smooth, adding some of the reserved cooking liquid or water until a medium consistency is reached.

4. Add the basil and roasted pepper and pulse until coarsely chopped; taste and adjust seasonings as needed.

5. Refrigerate and serve with European Peasant Bread (page 66) or Baguettes (page 50).

Tapenade Bread

We enjoy tapenade, the delightful French spread made from olives, anchovies and capers. This recipe was originally developed with a shop-bought tapenade, but then we started making our own. It was easy and had a freshness that the commercial product couldn't match. But if you have a jar of great tapenade on hand, by all means use it. This bread is great with cheeses or grilled with tomato, basil and garlic into mouth-watering Bruschetta (page 78).

Makes four 450g/1lb loaves. The recipe is easily doubled or halved.

The Tapenade (makes 225–450g/8oz–1lb)
• 225g/8oz pitted black olives
• 4 tsp capers, drained
• 4 anchovy fillets
• 1 garlic clove, put through a garlic press or very finely chopped
• ¼ tsp dried thyme
• 4 tbsp olive oil

The Dough
• 750ml/1¼ pints lukewarm water
• 1½ tbsp granulated yeast (decrease according to taste, see page 23)
• 1 tsp coarse grain salt (decrease according to taste, see page 25)
• 980g/1lb 3oz strong flour
• 225g/8oz home-made (above) or shop-bought tapenade
• Polenta or parchment paper for pizza peel, see page 29

1. Making the tapenade: coarsely chop all the tapenade ingredients together in a food processor. Set aside.

2. Mixing and storing the dough: mix the yeast and salt with the water in a 5 litre/8¾ pint bowl, or a lidded (not airtight) food container.

3. Mix in the remaining ingredients without kneading, using a spoon, a 3.5 litre/ 6 pint-capacity food processor (with dough attachment), or a heavy-duty stand mixer (with dough hook). If you're not using a machine, you may need to use wet hands to incorporate the last bit of flour.

4. Cover (not airtight), and allow to rest at room temperature until the dough rises and collapses (or flattens on top), approximately 2 hours.

5. The dough can be used immediately after the initial rise, though it is easier to handle when cold. Refrigerate in a lidded (not airtight) container and use over the next 7 days.

6. On baking day, dust the surface of the refrigerated dough with flour and cut off a 450g/1lb (grapefruit-size) piece. Dust the piece with more flour and quickly shape it into a ball by stretching the surface of the dough around to the bottom on all four sides, rotating the ball a quarter turn as you go. Allow to rest and rise on a polenta-covered pizza peel for 1 hour.

7. Thirty minutes before baking time, preheat the oven to 230°C/gas mark 8, with a baking stone placed on the middle rack (consider a longer preheat if you're finding your results to be denser than you like, see page 34). Place an empty grill tray on any other shelf that won't interfere with the rising bread.

8. Sprinkle the loaf liberally with flour and slash a deep cross, scallop or criss-cross pattern into the top, using a serrated bread knife. Leave the flour in place for baking; tap some of it off before eating.

9. Slide the loaf directly onto the hot stone. Pour 250ml/8 fl oz of hot tap water into the grill tray, and quickly close the oven door. Bake 35 to 40 minutes, or until deeply browned and firm. Smaller or larger loaves will require adjustments in baking time.

10. Allow to cool before slicing or eating.

Bruschetta

Here's one more way to use stale bread, which, like Panzanella (page 68), also comes from Italy. The Italians continually rearrange and reconstruct a limited number of delicious ingredients: bread, tomato, garlic, olive oil and herbs. Every family seems to have its own take on the combo.

'This was first made for me by my friend Marco, who was a visiting student from Livorno in Italy. He wanted to show off his family specialties, so he made a pasta dish with Parmigiano-Reggiano that he'd carried from Italy in his luggage, and to accompany it, this simple but memorable bruschetta.' – Jeff

Makes 4 bruschette starters.

• 4 thick slices of day-old Tapenade Bread (page 76),
  French Boule (page 44), or other non-enriched bread
• 1 garlic clove, cut in half
• 200g/7oz seeded and chopped tomato, well drained
• 8 torn or chopped fresh basil leaves
• Coarse grain salt
• 4 tsp extra virgin olive oil

1. Preheat the oven to 200°C/gas mark 6.
   Toast the bread slices until nicely crisp
   and browned.

2. Rub the pieces on both sides with the cut
   flat sides of the garlic. This will actually grate
   the raw garlic down into the toasted bread.
   Rub as much or as little as you like.

3. Place the bruschette on a baking sheet and
   top with the tomato, basil and a sprinkling of
   coarse grain salt. Finish with a liberal drizzling
   of olive oil; about a teaspoon per slice.

4. Bake for about 5 minutes, or until hot.
   Serve as an appetiser.

Deli-Style Rye

This loaf, our version of a classic sourdough rye, started Jeff's 20-year obsession with bread baking. The method produces a traditional rye comparable to those made with complicated starters – the kind that need to be 'fed', incubated and kept alive in your fridge. It makes a very nice loaf to eat on day one, but will be even better on day two or three. It is great with butter and it is perfect for our Reuben Sandwich (page 83).

Along with the caraway seeds, which give this bread its classic flavour, what sets this rye apart from other rustic breads is that there is no flour on the top crust; instead it's glazed with a cornflour wash, which serves the triple function of anchoring the caraway seeds, allowing the slashing knife to pass easily without sticking, and giving the loaf a beautiful shine.

'My grandmother truly did believe that this rye bread was better than cake. It turns out that elder immigrants from all over Europe felt the same way about "a good piece of bread." Friends of Dutch and Scandinavian heritage also recall older immigrant relatives shunning ordinary desserts in favour of extraordinary bread.' – Jeff

Makes four 450g/1lb loaves. The recipe is easily doubled or halved.

- 750ml/1¼ pints lukewarm water
- 1½ tbsp granulated yeast (decrease according to taste, see page 23)
- 1½ tbsp coarse grain salt (decrease according to taste, see page 25)
- 1½ tbsp caraway seeds, plus more for sprinkling on the top
- 140g/5oz rye flour
- 770g/1lb 11oz unbleached plain flour
- Polenta or parchment paper for pizza peel, see page 29
- Cornflour wash (see box, page 73)

1. Mixing and storing the dough: mix the yeast, salt and caraway seeds with the water in a 5 litre/8¾ pint bowl, or a lidded (not airtight) food container.

2. Mix in the remaining dry ingredients without kneading, using a spoon, a 3.5 litre/6 pint-capacity food processor (with dough attachment), or a heavy-duty stand mixer (with dough hook). If you're not using a machine, you may need to use wet hands to incorporate the last bit of flour.

3. Cover (not airtight), and allow to rest at room temperature until the dough rises and collapses (or flattens on top), approximately 2 hours.

4. The dough can be used immediately after the initial rise, though it is easier to handle when cold. Refrigerate in a lidded (not airtight) container and use over the next 14 days.

5. On baking day, dust the surface of the refrigerated dough with flour and cut off a 450g/1lb (grapefruit-size) piece. Dust the piece with more flour and quickly shape it into a ball by stretching the surface of the dough around to the bottom on all four sides, rotating the ball a quarter turn as you go. Elongate the ball into an oval-shaped loaf. Allow to rest and rise on a polenta-covered pizza peel for 40 minutes (consider a longer rest time if you're finding your results to be denser than you like, see page 39).

6. Thirty minutes before baking time, preheat the oven to 230°C/gas mark 8, with a baking stone placed on the middle rack (consider a longer preheat if you're finding your results to be denser than you like, see page 34). Place an empty grill tray on any other shelf that won't interfere with the rising bread.

7. Using a pastry brush, paint the top crust with cornflour wash and then sprinkle with additional caraway seeds. Slash with deep parallel cuts across the loaf, using a serrated bread knife.

8. Slide the loaf directly onto the hot stone. Pour 250ml/8 fl oz of hot tap water into the grill tray, and quickly close the oven door. Bake for about 30 minutes, or until deeply browned and firm. Smaller or larger loaves will require adjustments in baking time.

9. Allow to cool before slicing or eating.

Caraway Swirl Rye

This bread has a pleasing appearance and taste that will really appeal to caraway lovers. An extra dose of caraway is swirled through the bread, producing a beautiful and flavourful crunch.

Makes 1 caraway swirl rye.

- 450g/1lb (grapefruit-size portion) Deli-Style Rye dough (page 80)
- 2 tbsp caraway seeds, plus more for sprinkling on the top
- Polenta or parchment paper for pizza peel, see page 29
- Cornflour wash (see page 73)

1. Dust the surface of the refrigerated dough with flour and cut off a 450g/1lb (grapefruit-size) piece. Dust the piece with more flour and quickly shape it into a ball by stretching the surface of the dough around to the bottom on all four sides, rotating the ball a quarter turn as you go. Using your hands and a rolling pin, flatten the ball into a 1cm/½in-thick oval (avoid using extra flour here or it might remain as a dry deposit in the caraway swirl).

2. Sprinkle the dough with caraway seeds. The amount can vary with your taste; save some for the top crust. Then roll up the dough from the short end like a Swiss roll, forming a cylindrical loaf. Pinch the ends closed.

3. Allow to rest for 1 hour and 20 minutes (or just 40 minutes if you're using fresh, unrefrigerated dough).

4. Thirty minutes before baking time, preheat the oven to 230°C/gas mark 8, with a baking stone placed on the middle rack (consider a longer preheat if you're finding your results to be denser than you like, see page 34). Place an empty grill tray on any other shelf that won't interfere with the rising bread.

5. Using a pastry brush, paint the top crust with cornflour wash and then sprinkle with the additional caraway seeds. Slash with deep parallel cuts across the loaf, using a serrated bread knife.

6. Slide the loaf directly onto the hot stone. Pour 250ml/8 fl oz of hot tap water into the grill tray, and quickly close the oven door. Bake for 30 to 35 minutes, or until deeply browned and firm. Smaller or larger loaves will require adjustments in baking time.

7. Allow to cool before slicing or eating.

Reuben Sandwich

This sandwich is the king of the all-American delicatessen: home-baked rye bread (page 80) grilled in butter, dripping with rich cheese and Thousand Island dressing, piled high with corned beef. It towers above the common sandwich. But Reuben's no snob, so lose the wine – cold beer is the perfect accompaniment.

Makes 1 sandwich

- 1 tsp butter, plus more if needed
- 2 slices rye or pumpernickel bread
- 2 tsp Thousand Island dressing
- 25g/1oz thinly sliced Emmenthal cheese
- 50g/2oz thinly sliced corned beef
- 2 tbsp well-drained sauerkraut

1. Butter 1 side of each slice of bread. Place 1 slice of bread, butterside down, in a frying pan. Spread 1 teaspoon of Thousand Island dressing on the face-up side of the bread.

2. Cover with half the cheese, then the corned beef and sauerkraut. Finish with the other half of the cheese.

3. Spread the remaining Thousand Island dressing on the dry side of the second slice of bread to complete the sandwich.

4. Place the frying pan over medium-low heat and fry slowly for approximately 4 minutes per side, or until browned and crisp. Add additional butter to the pan if needed.

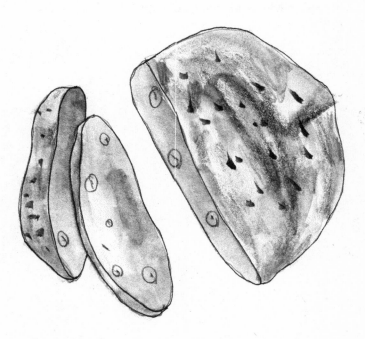

Onion Rye

The sweetness and aroma of sautéed onion go well with the flavour of rye. The onion needs to be sautéed until brown to bring out the caramelisation that makes this bread so interesting. This recipe can be made using the standard Deli-Style Rye (page 80), with or without caraway seeds. Ordinary yellow or white onions work well and are readily available, but red varieties produce a milder onion flavour that some will prefer.

Makes 1 onion rye.

Use any of these refrigerated pre-mixed doughs:
Deli-Style Rye (page 80) or Pumpernickel (page 88).

- 450g/1lb (grapefruit-size portion) of any pre-mixed dough listed above
- 1 medium onion, halved and sliced thinly
- Vegetable oil for sautéing the onions
- Polenta or parchment paper for pizza peel, see page 29
- Cornflour wash (see box, page 73)

1. Sauté the onions in the oil over medium heat for 10 minutes, or until brown.

2. Dust the surface of the refrigerated dough with flour and cut off a 450g/1lb (grapefruit-size) piece of dough. Dust the piece with more flour and quickly shape it into a ball by stretching the surface of the dough around to the bottom on all four sides, rotating the ball a quarter turn as you go. Flatten the ball into a 1cm/½in-thick oval either with your hands or a rolling pin (avoid using much extra flour here or it might remain as a dry deposit).

3. Spread the surface of the flattened loaf with a thin layer of the browned onion. Then roll up the dough from the short end like a Swiss roll, forming a log.

4. Allow to rest and rise for 1 hour and 20 minutes (or just 40 minutes if you're using fresh, unrefrigerated dough).

5. Thirty minutes before baking time, preheat the oven to 230°C/gas mark 8, with a baking stone placed on the middle rack (consider a longer preheat if you're finding your results to be denser than you like, see page 34). Place an empty grill tray on any other shelf that won't interfere with the rising bread.

6. Using a pastry brush, paint the top crust with cornflour wash. Slash with deep parallel cuts across the loaf, using a serrated bread knife.

7. Slide the loaf directly onto the hot stone. Pour 250ml/8 fl oz of hot tap water into the grill tray, and quickly close the oven door. Bake for 30 to 35 minutes, until deeply browned and firm. Smaller or larger loaves will require adjustments in baking time.

8. Allow to cool before slicing or eating.

Limpa

Here's a five-minutes-a-day version of a traditional Scandinavian comfort food. Honey and orange zest blend with the more exotic flavours of anise and cardamom in this delicious Swedish bread.

Make two loaves; the first loaf will go quickly and you can use the second one in our bread pudding recipe, page 246.

Makes four 450g/1lb loaves. The recipe is easily doubled or halved.

- 750ml/1¼ pints lukewarm water
- 1½ tbsp granulated yeast (decrease according to taste, see page 23)
- 1½ tbsp coarse grain salt (decrease according to taste, see page 25)
- 8 tbsp clear honey
- ½ tsp ground anise seed
- 1 tsp ground cardamom
- 1½ tsp orange zest
- 140g/5oz rye flour
- 770g/1lb 11oz unbleached plain flour
- Cornflour wash (see box, page 73)
- Additionally, for each finished loaf you'll need ¼ tsp ground anise seed, ¼ tsp ground cardamom, plus 1½ tsp sugar mixed together for sprinkling on the top crust
- Wholemeal flour or parchment paper for pizza peel, see page 29

1. Mixing and storing the dough: mix the yeast, salt, honey, spices and orange zest with the water in a 5 litre/8¾ pint bowl, or a lidded (not airtight) food container.

2. Mix in the remaining dry ingredients without kneading, using a spoon, a 3.5 litre/6 pint-capacity food processor (with dough attachment), or a heavy-duty stand mixer (with dough hook). If you're not using a machine, you may need to use wet hands to incorporate the last bit of flour.

3. Cover (not airtight), and allow to rest at room temperature until dough rises and collapses (or flattens on top), approximately 2 hours.

4. The dough can be used immediately after the initial rise, though it is easier to handle when cold. Refrigerate in a lidded (not airtight) container and use over the next 7 days.

5. On baking day, dust the surface of the refrigerated dough with flour and cut off a 450g/1lb (grapefruit-size) piece. Dust the piece with more flour and quickly shape it into a ball by stretching the surface of the dough around to the bottom on all four sides, rotating the ball a quarter turn as you go. Allow to rest and rise on a wholemeal-covered pizza peel for 40 minutes (consider a longer rest time if you're finding your results to be denser than you like, see page 39).

6. Thirty minutes before baking time, preheat the oven to 190°C/gas mark 5, with a baking stone placed on the middle rack (consider a longer preheat if you're finding your results to be denser than you like, see page 34). Place an empty grill tray on any other shelf that won't interfere with the rising bread.

7. Paint the surface with cornflour wash and slash a deep cross, scallop or criss-cross pattern into the top, using a serrated bread knife. Sprinkle with the additional anise, cardamom and sugar mixture.

8. Slide the loaf directly onto the hot stone. Pour 250ml/8 fl oz of hot tap water into the grill tray, and quickly close the oven door. Bake for about 40 minutes, or until golden brown and firm. Smaller or larger loaves will require adjustments in baking time. Due to the honey, the crust on this bread will not be hard and crackling.

9. Allow to cool before slicing or eating.

Pumpernickel Bread

Pumpernickel bread is really just a variety of rye bread. What darkens the loaf and accounts for its mildly bitter but appealing flavour is cocoa, molasses and coffee, not the flour. Very traditional recipes use pumpernickel flour (a coarse rye with lots of rye bran), but this grain doesn't do well in our recipes because it absorbs water unpredictably. Since it's really the coffee and chocolate that give pumpernickel its unique flavour and colour, we successfully created a pumpernickel bread without true pumpernickel flour.

This bread is associated with Russia and caviar. If you're partial to caviar, here's your chance. Or just pile on the pastrami and corned beef!

Makes four 450g/1lb loaves. The recipe is easily doubled or halved.

- 750ml/1¼ pints lukewarm water
- 1½ tbsp granulated yeast (decrease according to taste, see page 23)
- 1½ tbsp coarse grain salt (decrease according to taste, see page 25)
- 2 tbsp molasses
- 1½ tbsp cocoa powder
- 2 tsp instant espresso powder or instant coffee (or substitute brewed coffee for 475ml/16 fl oz of the water, keeping the total volume at 750ml/1¼ pints)
- 140g/5oz rye flour
- 770g/1lb 11oz unbleached plain flour
- Polenta or parchment paper for pizza peel, see page 29
- Whole caraway seeds for sprinkling on the top, optional
- Cornflour wash (see box, page 73)

1. Mixing and storing the dough: mix the yeast, salt, molasses, cocoa and espresso powder with the water in a 5 litre/8¾ pint bowl, or a lidded (not airtight) food container.

2. Mix in the flours without kneading, using a spoon, a 3.5 litre/6 pint-capacity food processor (with dough attachment), or a heavy-duty stand mixer (with dough hook). If you're not using a machine, you may need to use wet hands to incorporate the last bit of flour.

3. Cover (not airtight), and allow to rest at room temperature until the dough rises and collapses (or flattens on top), approximately 2 hours.

4. The dough can be used immediately after the initial rise, though it is easier to handle when cold. Refrigerate in a lidded (not airtight) container and use over the next 8 days.

5. On baking day, cut off a 450g/1lb (grapefruit-size) piece of dough. Using wet hands (don't use flour), quickly shape the dough into a ball by stretching the surface of the dough around to the bottom on all four sides, rotating the ball a quarter turn as you go. Then form an oval-shaped loaf. Allow to rest and rise on a polenta-covered pizza peel for 40 minutes (consider a longer rest time if you're finding your results to be denser than you like, see page 39).

6. Thirty minutes before baking time, preheat the oven to 200°C/gas mark 6, with a baking stone placed on the middle rack (consider a longer preheat if you're finding your results to be denser than you like, see page 34). Place an empty grill tray on any other shelf that won't interfere with the rising bread.

7. Using a pastry brush, paint the top crust with cornflour wash and sprinkle with the caraway seeds, if using. Slash the loaf with deep parallel cuts, using a serrated bread knife.

8. Slide the loaf directly onto the hot stone. Pour 250ml/8 fl oz of hot tap water into the grill tray, and quickly close the oven door. Bake for 35 to 40 minutes, until firm. Smaller or larger loaves will require adjustments in baking time.

9. Allow to cool before slicing or eating.

Altus

Many traditional pumpernickel recipes call for the addition of 'altus', which is stale rye or pumpernickel bread crumbs, soaked in water and blended into the dough. If you want to find a use for some stale rye or pumpernickel bread, you can experiment with this approach, which some say adds moisture and flavour to many traditional rye breads. Add up to 50g/2oz to the liquid ingredients before the flours. Adjust the flours to end up with dough of your usual consistency.

Pumpernickel Date and Walnut Bread

The sweetness of the dried fruit and the richness of the nuts are wonderful with the aromatic pumpernickel dough. We finish this loaf with nothing but the traditional cornflour wash, letting the flavour of the fruit and nuts come through.

Makes 1 loaf.

- 450g/1lb (grapefruit-size portion) Pumpernickel Bread dough (page 88)
- 25g/1oz chopped walnuts
- 40g/1½oz chopped dates or raisins
- Polenta or parchment paper for pizza peel, see page 29
- Cornflour wash (see box, page 73)

1. On baking day, using wet hands instead of flour, cut off a 450g/1lb (grapefruit-size) piece of dough. Continuing with wet hands, quickly shape the dough into a ball by stretching the surface of the dough around to the bottom on all four sides, rotating the ball a quarter turn as you go.

2. Flatten the dough with your wet hands to a thickness of 1cm/½in and sprinkle with the walnuts and dates. Roll up the dough from the short end, like a Swiss roll, to form a log. Using wet hands, crimp the ends shut and tuck them under to form an oval loaf.

3. Allow to rest and rise on a polenta-covered pizza peel for 1 hour and 40 minutes (or just 40 minutes if you're using fresh, unrefrigerated dough).

4. Thirty minutes before baking time, preheat the oven to 200°C/gas mark 6, with a baking stone placed on the middle rack (consider a longer preheat if you're finding your results to be denser than you like, see page 34). Place an empty grill tray on any other shelf that won't interfere with the rising bread.

5. Using a pastry brush, paint the top crust with cornflour wash and then slash the loaf with deep parallel cuts, using a serrated bread knife.

6. Slide the loaf directly onto the hot stone. Pour 250ml/8 fl oz of hot tap water into the grill tray, and quickly close the oven door. Bake for 35 to 40 minutes, until firm. Smaller or larger loaves will require adjustments in baking time.

7. Allow to cool before slicing or eating.

Bran-Enriched White Bread

There's no point in belabouring the value of bran in the diet. Weight for weight, wheat bran is much higher in fibre than wholemeal flour, yet it doesn't change the taste of bread as much as wholemeal flour. For those who don't care for the pleasantly bitter, nutty flavour of wholemeal, this loaf can serve as a mild-tasting, high-fibre substitute.

Makes four 450g/1lb loaves. The recipe is easily doubled or halved.

- 750ml/1¼ pints lukewarm water
- 1½ tbsp granulated yeast (decrease according to taste, see page 23)
- 1½ tbsp coarse grain salt (decrease according to taste, see page 25)
- 130g/4½oz wheat bran
- 800g/1¾lb unbleached plain flour
- Polenta or parchment paper for pizza peel, see page 29
- Cornflour wash (see box, page 73)

1. Mixing and storing the dough: mix the yeast and salt with the water in a 5 litre/8¾ pint bowl, or a lidded (not airtight) food container.

2. Mix in the remaining dry ingredients without kneading, using a spoon, a 3.5 litre/6 pint-capacity food processor (with dough attachment), or a heavy-duty stand mixer (with dough hook). If you're not using a machine, you may need to use wet hands to incorporate the last bit of flour.

3. Allow to rest at room temperature until the dough rises and collapses (or flattens on top), approximately 2 hours.

4. The dough can be used immediately after the initial rise, though it is easier to handle when cold. Refrigerate in a lidded (not airtight) container and use over the next 14 days.

5. On baking day, dust the surface of the refrigerated dough with flour and cut off a 450g/1lb (grapefruit-size) piece. Dust the piece with more flour and quickly shape it into a ball by stretching the surface of the dough around to the bottom on all four sides, rotating the ball a quarter turn as you go. Then form an oval-shaped loaf. Allow to rest and rise on a polenta-covered pizza peel for 40 minutes (consider a longer rest time if you're finding your results to be denser than you like, see page 39).

6. Thirty minutes before baking time, preheat the oven to 230°C/gas mark 8, with a baking stone placed on the middle rack (consider a longer preheat if you're finding your results to be denser than you like, see page 34). Place an empty grill tray on any other shelf that won't interfere with the rising bread.

7. Sprinkle the loaf liberally with flour and slash parallel cuts across the loaf, using a serrated bread knife. Leave the flour in place for baking; tap some of it off before eating.

8. Slide the loaf directly onto the hot stone. Pour 250ml/8 fl oz of hot tap water into the grill tray, and quickly close the oven door. Bake for about 30 minutes, until deeply browned and firm. Smaller or larger loaves will require adjustments in baking time.

9. Allow to cool before slicing or eating.

Light Wholemeal Bread

You'll find this recipe a basic workhorse when you want a versatile and healthy light wheat bread for sandwiches, appetisers and snacks. The blend of plain flour and wholemeal creates a bread lighter in texture, taste and appearance than our 100% Wholemeal (page 96). Try them both and find your favourite.

Makes four 450g/1lb loaves. The recipe is easily doubled or halved.

- 750ml/1¼ pints lukewarm water
- 1½ tbsp granulated yeast (decrease according to taste, see page 23)
- 1½ tbsp coarse grain salt (decrease according to taste, see page 25)
- 140g/5oz wholemeal flour
- 770g/1lb 11oz unbleached plain flour
- Wholemeal flour or parchment paper for pizza peel, see page 29

1. Mixing and storing the dough: mix the yeast and salt with the water in a 5 litre/8¾ pint bowl, or a lidded (not airtight) food container.

2. Mix in the remaining dry ingredients without kneading, using a spoon, a 3.5 litre/6 pint-capacity food processor (with dough attachment), or a heavy-duty stand mixer (with dough hook). If you're not using a machine, you may need to use wet hands to incorporate the last bit of flour.

3. Cover (not airtight), and allow to rest at room temperature until the dough rises and collapses (or flattens on top), approximately 2 hours.

4. The dough can be used immediately after the initial rise, though it is easier to handle when cold. Refrigerate in a lidded (not airtight) container and use over the next 14 days.

5. On baking day, dust the surface of the refrigerated dough with flour and cut off a 450g/1lb (grapefruit-size) piece. Dust the piece with more flour and quickly shape it into a ball by stretching the surface of the dough around to the bottom on all four sides, rotating the ball a quarter turn as you go. Allow to rest and rise on a flour-covered pizza peel or 40 minutes (consider a longer rest time if you're finding your results to be denser than you like, see page 39).

6. Thirty minutes before baking time, preheat the oven to 230°C/gas mark 8, with a baking stone placed on the middle rack (consider a longer preheat if you're finding your results to be denser than you like, see page 34). Place an empty grill tray on any other shelf that won't interfere with the rising bread.

7. Sprinkle the loaf liberally with flour and slash a deep cross, scallop or criss-cross pattern into the top, using a serrated bread knife. Leave the flour in place for baking; tap some of it off before eating.

8. Slide the loaf directly onto the hot stone. Pour 250ml/8 fl oz of hot tap water into the grill tray, and quickly close the oven door. Bake for about 35 minutes, or until deeply browned and firm. Smaller or larger loaves will require adjustments in baking time.

9. Allow to cool before slicing or eating.

100% Wholemeal Sandwich Bread

Wholemeal flour has a nutty, slightly bitter flavour, and it caramelises very easily, yielding a rich, brown and flavourful loaf. We've used milk and honey as tenderisers, but the honey's sweetness also makes a nice counterpoint to the wholemeal's bitter notes. Although we've showcased a loaf-tin method here, this dough also makes lovely free-form loaves using the baking stone.

Makes three 675g/1½lb loaves. The recipe is easily doubled or halved.

- 350ml/12 fl oz lukewarm water
- 350ml/12 fl oz lukewarm milk
- 1½ tbsp granulated yeast (decrease according to taste, see page 23)
- 1 tbsp plus 1 tsp coarse grain salt (decrease according to taste, see page 25)
- 8 tbsp clear honey
- 5 tbsp neutral-flavoured oil, plus more for greasing the tin
- 935g/2lb 1oz wholemeal flour

1. Mixing and storing the dough: mix the yeast, salt, honey and oil with the milk and water in a 5 litre/8¾ pint bowl, or a lidded (not airtight) food container.

2. Mix in the remaining dry ingredients without kneading, using a spoon, a 3.5 litre/6 pint-capacity food processor (with dough attachment), or a heavy-duty stand mixer (with dough hook).

3. Cover (not airtight), and allow to rest at room temperature until the dough rises and collapses (or flattens on top), approximately 2 to 3 hours.

4. The dough can be used immediately after the initial rise, though it is easier to handle when cold. Refrigerate in a lidded (not airtight) container and use over the next 5 days.

5. On baking day, lightly grease a 23 x 10 x 7.5cm/9 x 4 x 3in non-stick loaf tin. Using wet hands, scoop out a 675g/1½lb (cantaloupe-size) handful of dough. This dough is pretty sticky and often it's easiest to handle it with wet hands. Keeping your hands wet, quickly shape it into a ball by stretching the surface of the dough around to the bottom on all four sides, rotating the ball a quarter turn as you go.

6. Drop the loaf into the prepared tin. You want to fill the tin slightly more than half-full.

7. Allow the dough to rest for 1 hour and 40 minutes. Flour the top of the loaf and slash, using the tip of a serrated bread knife.

8. Thirty minutes before baking time, preheat the oven to 190°C/gas mark 5, with an empty grill tray on any other shelf that won't interfere with the rising bread. If you're not using a stone, the preheat can be as short as 5 minutes.

9. Place the loaf on a rack near the centre of the oven. Pour 250ml/8 fl oz of hot tap water into the grill tray and quickly close the oven door. Bake for 50 to 60 minutes, or until deeply browned and firm.

10. Allow to cool completely before slicing, in order to cut reasonable sandwich slices.

Wholemeal Sandwich Bread Inspired by Chris Kimball

Chris Kimball publishes *Cook's Magazine*, and has written a number of wonderful commonsense cookbooks celebrating American regional home cooking. As Chris has written, home chefs can produce honest and authentic but simple versions of what the best artisan chefs spend a lifetime perfecting. We agree, and that's part of the idea behind this book: authentic but simple.

In 1997, Chris developed a wholemeal bread recipe in the soft-crusted American style, and ran it in *Cook's Magazine*. We've adapted it here for stored high-moisture dough and we think you'll enjoy the delicious effect created by the wheat germ, rye and honey. Even though this bread is soft-crusted, we bake it with steam because it improves the colour and appearance.

Makes three 675g/1½lb loaves. The recipe is easily doubled or halved.

- 750ml/1¼ pints lukewarm water
- 1½ tbsp granulated yeast (decrease according to taste, see page 23)
- 1 tbsp plus 1 tsp coarse grain salt (decrease according to taste, see page 25)
- 3 tbsp clear honey
- 50g/2oz unsalted butter, melted
- 35g/1¼oz rye flour
- 75g/3oz wheat germ
- 385g/13½oz wholemeal flour
- 385g/13½oz unbleached plain flour
- Neutral-tasting oil for greasing the tin

1. Mixing and storing the dough: mix the yeast, salt, honey and butter with the lukewarm water in a 5 litre/8¾ pint bowl, or a lidded (not airtight) food container.

2. Mix in the remaining dry ingredients without kneading, using a spoon, a 3.5 litre/6 pint-capacity food processor (with dough attachment), or a heavy-duty stand mixer (with dough hook). If you're not using a machine, you may need to use wet hands to incorporate the last bit of flour.

3. Cover (not airtight), and allow to rest at room temperature until the dough rises and collapses (or flattens on top), approximately 2 hours.

4. The dough can be used immediately after the initial rise, though it is easier to handle when cold. Refrigerate in a lidded (not airtight) container and use over the next 5 days.

5. On baking day, lightly grease a 23 x 10 x 7.5cm/9 x 4 x 3in non-stick loaf tin. Dust the surface of the refrigerated dough with flour and cut off a 675g/1½lb (cantaloupe-size) piece. Dust the piece with more flour and quickly shape it into a ball by stretching the surface of the dough around to the bottom on all four sides, rotating the ball a quarter turn as you go. Form an elongated oval and place it into the prepared tin. Allow to rest for 1 hour and 40 minutes (or just 40 minutes if you're using fresh, unrefrigerated dough).

6. Thirty minutes before baking time, preheat the oven to 200°C/gas mark 6, with an empty grill tray on any other shelf that won't interfere with the rising bread. If you're not using a stone, the preheat can be as short as 5 minutes.

7. Place the loaf on a rack near the centre of the oven. Pour 250ml/8 fl oz of hot tap water into the grill tray and quickly close the oven door. Bake for about 50 minutes, or until deeply browned and firm.

8. Allow to cool before slicing or eating.

Italian Semolina Bread

White, free-form loaves flavoured with semolina and sesame seeds are the fragrant products of southern Italy. Semolina is a high-protein wheat flour that gives loaves a sweetness and an almost winey aroma. In our minds, the flavour of the sesame seeds is inextricably linked to the semolina flavour (like caraway and rye). Be sure to use semolina flour that's labelled 'durum'; other semolina flours won't do as well in our method.

Makes four 450g/1lb loaves. The recipe is easily doubled or halved.

- 750ml/1¼ pints lukewarm water
- 1½ tbsp granulated yeast (decrease according to taste, see page 23)
- 1½ tbsp coarse grain salt (decrease according to taste, see page 25)
- 420g/15oz semolina flour
- 450g/1lb unbleached plain flour
- Sesame seeds for top crust, approximately 1 to 2 tsp
- Polenta or parchment paper for pizza peel, see page 29
- Cornflour wash (see box, page 73)

1. Mixing and storing the dough: mix the yeast and salt with the lukewarm water in a 5 litre/8¾ pint bowl, or a lidded (not airtight) food container.

2. Mix in the flours without kneading, using a spoon, a 3.5 litre/6 pint-capacity food processor (with dough attachment), or a heavy-duty stand mixer (with dough hook). If you're not using a machine, you may need to use wet hands to incorporate the last bit of flour.

3. Cover (not airtight), and allow to rest at room temperature until the dough rises and collapses (or flattens on top), approximately 2 hours.

4. The dough can be used immediately after the initial rise, though it is easier to handle when cold. Refrigerate in a lidded (not airtight) container and use over the next 14 days.

5. On baking day, dust the surface of the refrigerated dough with flour and cut off a 450g/1lb (grapefruit-size) piece. Dust the piece with more flour and quickly shape it into a ball by stretching the surface of the dough around to the bottom on all four sides, rotating the ball a quarter turn as you go. Elongate the ball to form an oval-shaped free-form loaf. Allow to rest and rise on a polenta-covered pizza peel for 40 minutes (consider a longer rest time if you're finding your results to be denser than you like, see page 39).

6. Thirty minutes before baking time, preheat the oven to 230°C/gas mark 8, with a baking stone placed on the middle rack (consider a longer preheat if you're finding your results to be denser than you like, see page 34). Place an empty grill tray on any other shelf that won't interfere with the rising bread.

7. Just before baking, paint the surface with cornflour wash, sprinkle with sesame seeds and slash the surface diagonally, using a serrated bread knife.

8. Slide the loaf directly onto the hot stone. Pour 250ml/8 fl oz of hot tap water into the grill tray, and quickly close the oven door. Bake for 30 to 35 minutes, until deeply browned and firm. Smaller or larger loaves will require adjustments in baking time.

9. Allow to cool before slicing or eating.

Broa (Portuguese Corn Bread)

Broa is a very rustic recipe from the Portuguese countryside. It is a dense part-corn loaf that's perfect for sopping up hearty soups like our Portuguese Fish Stew (page 104). It bears little resemblance to American Southern cornbread, which is quite sweet, and leavened with bicarbonate of soda and baking powder.

Form this loaf as a relatively flattened ball (so that you'll get lots of crust). The flattened loaf is truer to the original and helps to prevent denseness from the corn.

Makes four 450g/1lb loaves. The recipe is easily doubled or halved.

- 750ml/1¼ pints lukewarm water
- 1½ tbsp granulated yeast (decrease according to taste, see page 23)
- 1½ tbsp coarse grain salt (decrease according to taste, see page 25)
- 175g/6oz polenta
- 700g/1lb 8oz unbleached plain flour
- Polenta for pizza peel and dusting the top

1. Mixing and storing the dough: mix the yeast and salt with the water in a 5 litre/8¾ pint bowl, or a lidded (not airtight) food container.

2. Mix in the remaining dry ingredients without kneading, using a spoon, a 3.5 litre/6 pint-capacity food processor (with dough attachment), or a heavy-duty stand mixer (with dough hook). If you're not using a machine, you may need to use wet hands to incorporate the last bit of flour.

3. Cover (not airtight), and allow to rest at room temperature until the dough rises and collapses (or flattens on top), approximately 2 hours.

4. The dough can be used immediately after the initial rise, though it is easier to handle when cold. Refrigerate in a lidded (not airtight) container and use over the next 10 days.

5. On baking day, dust the surface of the refrigerated dough with flour and cut off a 450g/1lb (grapefruit-size) piece. Dust the piece with more flour and quickly shape it into a ball by stretching the surface of the dough around to the bottom on all four sides, rotating the ball a quarter turn as you go. Flatten slightly and allow to rest and rise on a polenta-covered pizza peel for 40 minutes (consider a longer rest time if you're finding your results to be denser than you like, see page 39).

6. Thirty minutes before baking time, preheat the oven to 230°C/gas mark 8, with a baking stone placed on the middle rack. Place an empty grill tray on any other shelf that won't interfere with the rising bread.

7. Just before baking, sprinkle the loaf liberally with polenta and slash a deep cross, scallop or criss-cross pattern into the top, using a serrated bread knife. Leave the polenta in place for baking; tap some of it off before eating.

8. Slide the loaf directly onto the hot stone. Pour 250ml/8 fl oz of hot tap water into the grill tray, and quickly close the oven door. Bake for about 30 minutes, until deeply browned and firm. Smaller or larger loaves will require adjustments in baking time.

9. Allow to cool before slicing or eating.

Portuguese Fish Stew
(Caldeirada de Peixe)

We include this simple and delicious recipe that was born to have Broa (page 102) dipped into it. The distinguishing character of this soup comes from the orange zest and hot chilli flakes, which makes it quite different from French or Italian versions. Cod is a typical Portuguese choice to include, but the dish works well with any combination of boneless white-fleshed, non-oily fish and/or shellfish.

Makes 6 to 8 servings.

- 3 tbsp olive oil
- 1 large onion, chopped
- 2 leeks, washed to remove interior soil and coarsely chopped
- 1 bulb fennel, white parts only, coarsely chopped
- 5 garlic cloves, finely chopped
- 115g/4oz canned or fresh tomatoes, diced
- 1 red pepper, cored, seeded and diced
- 1 bay leaf
- Zest of 1 orange
- 1 litre/1¾ pints fish stock or water
- 475ml/16 fl oz dry white wine
- Scant ¼ tsp dried chilli flakes
- 1 tbsp salt (decrease according to taste, see page 25)
- Freshly ground pepper to taste
- 1.3kg/3lb mixed white, non-oily boneless fish and shellfish, or just fish

1. Heat the oil in a large pan, add the onion and leeks, and sauté until softened. Add the fennel and garlic and sauté until aromatic.

2. Add all the remaining ingredients except the fish and shellfish and bring to a boil. Cover, lower heat and simmer for 20 minutes.

3. While the stock is simmering, cut the fish into bite-size portions. Bring the stock back to a rapid boil, add the fish and cook for 1 minute.

4. Add the shellfish (if using) and continue to boil until shells open, approximately 1 minute. Shake the pan occasionally to encourage clam and mussel shells to open. If using prawns, turn off the heat as soon as all the prawns lose their gray translucency; any longer and they quickly become tough and overcooked. Depending on your pan and hob, this will probably be about 2 to 3 minutes.

5. Serve hot with wedges of Broa.

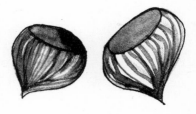

Yeasted Thanksgiving Corn Bread with Cranberries

Traditional American corn bread is a butter or lard-enriched quick bread, risen with baking powder and bicarbonate of soda. We make ours with yeasted Broa dough (page 102). For a Thanksgiving feel, we studded the dough with sweetened cranberries. Playing on the American corn-bread theme, we baked the loaf in a heated cast-iron pan, liberally greased with butter, lard, bacon fat or oil, creating a rich and flavourful crust.

Like a baking stone, cast iron absorbs a lot of energy when its temperature rises in an oven, retains heat well and radiates it very evenly to the dough, promoting a nice brown crust. Though cast iron can't absorb moisture, it makes the baking stone optional here.

Makes 1 corn bread.

- 675g/1½lb Broa dough (page 102) approximately 1 cantaloupe-size handful, or enough to fill a 30cm/12in cast-iron pan to a depth of about 4cm/1½in
- 50g/2oz fresh or dried cranberries
- 4 tbsp sugar
- Zest of half an orange
- 3 tbsp softened butter, lard, bacon fat or neutral-tasting oil for greasing the tin

1. Dust the surface of the refrigerated dough with flour and cut off a 675g/1½lb (cantaloupe-size) piece. Dust the piece with more flour and quickly shape it into a ball by stretching the surface of the dough around to the bottom on all four sides, rotating the ball a quarter turn as you go.

2. Flatten the ball with your hands to a thickness of 1cm/½in. Sprinkle the dough with the cranberries, sugar and orange zest. Roll up the dough from the short end, Swiss roll style, to incorporate the cranberries. Shape into a ball again, then flatten until it is about the size of your pan.

3. Grease a cast-iron pan with all of the butter, lard, bacon fat or oil, being sure to coat the sides of the pan as well. Place the dough into the pan. Allow the dough to rest for 1 hour and 20 minutes (or just 40 minutes if you're using fresh, unrefrigerated dough).

4. Thirty minutes before baking time, preheat the oven to 220°C/gas mark 7, and place a grill tray for water on any other shelf that won't interfere with the rising bread (consider a longer preheat if you're finding your results to be denser than you like, see page 34). A baking stone is optional here given the use of a castiron pan. If you omit the stone, the preheat can be as short as 5 minutes.

5. Just before baking, heat the cast-iron pan over medium heat for 1 or 2 minutes to jump-start the baking process and promote caramelisation of the bottom crust (don't overdo it – no more than 2 minutes).

6. Place the pan on a rack near the centre of the oven. Pour 250ml/8 fl oz of hot tap water into the grill tray and quickly close the oven door. Check for browning in about 20 minutes. The time required will depend on the size and weight of pan but will probably be about 30 minutes. The loaf should be a rich yellow-brown when done.

7. Carefully turn the hot loaf out of the pan onto a serving plate, or just cut wedges directly out of the pan.

Spicy Pork Buns

We'd been searching for a simple way to re-create and reconstruct some of the flavour combinations in great tamales. Here's a simple recipe combining the sweet flavour of corn from the Broa dough, meat and two kinds of chilli peppers. It's a bit more time-consuming than our other recipes, but worth it.

Children devour these, but if your kids won't eat spicy food, you may want to tone down the chipotles en adobo, or leave them out altogether. We serve this dish as a main course, with added sauce on the side. You can put more sauce inside the buns, but don't overdo it or the result may be soggy.

Makes 4 large buns.

The Meat Filling
- 150–225g/5–8oz cooked roast pork or beef
- 800g crushed tomato passata
- 2 chipotle peppers from a can of chipotles en adobo, finely chopped
- 2 dried chillies or 1 tbsp of your favourite chilli powder
- 1 medium onion
- 1½ tsp cumin seeds
- 2 tsp salt (decrease according to taste, see page 25)
- 1 tsp cornflour
- 2 tbsp chopped fresh coriander

The Wrappers
- 450g/1lb (grapefruit-size portion) Broa dough (page 102)

1. Make the meat filling: if you're grinding your own chillies, briefly toast the dried peppers in a 200°C/gas mark 6 oven until fragrant but not burned, 1 to 2 minutes (they'll remain flexible). Break up the toasted chillies and discard the stems and seeds. Grind with the cumin seeds in a spice grinder (or coffee grinder used just for spices).

2. Trim the meat of hardened fat; shred with knife, fork and your fingers, pulling strips off the meat along the direction of the grain.

3. Place all ingredients for the meat filling except the cornflour and coriander in a roomy pan on the hob. The liquid should not come higher than about one-third of the way up the meat. Bring to a simmer and cook, covered, until very soft, approximately 3 hours, turning occasionally. Separate the meat and sauce and chill in the fridge.

4. When chilled, skim the fat from the surface of the sauce. Anytime before assembling the buns, reheat the meat mixture. Mix the cornflour with a small amount of sauce in a little cup to make a paste; then add to the pot. Simmer for 2 minutes, or until thickened.

5. Preheat the oven to 230°C/gas mark 8, with a baking stone set in the middle of the oven. Place a grill tray for holding water on any other shelf that won't interfere with the rising bread.

6. Dust the surface of the refrigerated dough with flour and cut off a 450g/1lb (grapefruit-size) piece. Divide the dough into four equal balls. Briefly shape, flattening out each ball with your fingers. Using a rolling pin, roll out 20–25cm/8–10in rounds about 3mm/⅛in thick or less. Use minimal white flour on your work surface as you roll so that the dough sticks to it a bit.

7. Assemble the buns: place approximately 4 tablespoons of shredded meat in the centre of each round of dough. Add about a tablespoon of sauce and ½ tablespoon of chopped coriander. Wet the edges of the dough round with water. Gather the edges of the dough around the meat, pinching at the centre to form a seal; you may need to use a dough scraper to pull up sections of the wrapper.

8. Using a dough scraper, if necessary, remove the finished buns from the work surface and place on a polenta-covered pizza peel. No resting time is needed.

9. Slide the buns directly onto the hot stone. Pour 250ml/8 fl oz of hot tap water into the grill tray, and quickly close the oven door. Check for browning in 15 minutes and continue baking until the buns are medium brown.

10. Serve immediately, with additional sauce, and Mexican hot pepper sauce.

English Granary-Style Bread

When it comes to English bread, we're traditionalists. Here is a staple of the old village bakery: a multigrain loaf that includes malted wheat and barley. The combination of grains create a slightly sweet and comforting flavour.

Makes four 450g/1lb loaves. The recipe is easily doubled or halved.

- 850ml/27 fl oz lukewarm water
- 1½ tbsp granulated yeast (decrease according to taste, see page 23)
- 1½ tbsp coarse grain salt (decrease according to taste, see page 25)
- 25g/1oz malt powder
- 90g/3½oz malted wheat flakes
- 140g/5oz wholemeal flour
- 700g/1lb 8oz unbleached plain flour
- Polenta or parchment paper for pizza peel, see page 29
- Cornflour wash (see box, page 73)
- 1 tbsp cracked wheat, for sprinkling on top crust

1. Mixing and storing the dough: mix the yeast, salt and malt powder with the lukewarm water in a 5 litre/8¾ pint bowl, or a lidded (not airtight) food container.

2. Mix in the wheat flakes and the flours without kneading, using a spoon, a 3.5 litre/ 6 pint-capacity food processor (with dough attachment), or a heavy-duty stand mixer (with dough hook). If you're not using a machine, you may need to use wet hands to incorporate the last bit of flour.

3. Cover (not airtight), and allow to rest at room temperature until the dough rises and collapses (or flattens on top), approximately 2 hours.

4. The dough can be used immediately after the initial rise, though it is easier to handle when cold. Refrigerate in a lidded (not airtight) container and use over the next 10 days.

5. On baking day, dust the surface of the refrigerated dough with flour and cut off a 450g/1lb (grapefruit-size) piece. Dust the piece with more flour and quickly shape it into a ball by stretching the surface of the dough around to the bottom on all four sides, rotating the ball a quarter turn as you go. Allow to rest and rise on a polenta-covered pizza peel for 40 minutes (consider a longer rest time if you're finding your results to be denser than you like, see page 39).

6. Thirty minutes before baking time, preheat the oven to 200°C/gas mark 6, with a baking stone placed on the middle rack (consider a longer preheat if you're finding your results to be denser than you like, see page 34). Place an empty grill tray on any other shelf that won't interfere with the rising bread.

7. Brush the loaf with cornflour wash and sprinkle with cracked wheat. Slash a cross or a criss-cross pattern into the top, using a serrated bread knife.

8. Slide the loaf directly onto the hot stone. Pour 250ml/8 fl oz of hot tap water into the grill tray, and quickly close the oven door. Bake for about 35 minutes. Smaller or larger loaves will require adjustments in baking time.

9. Allow to cool before slicing.

Oatmeal Bread

This lightly sweetened and hearty bread tastes great straight from the oven with butter and cinnamon sugar. It also makes a great sandwich with smoked turkey and cheese. Or serve it with Laura's Three Citrus Marmalade (page 114).

Makes three 675g/1½lb loaves. The recipe is easily doubled or halved.

- 400ml/14 fl oz lukewarm water
- 250ml/8 fl oz whole milk
- 120ml/4 fl oz pure maple syrup
- 1½ tbsp granulated yeast (decrease according to taste, see page 23)
- 1 tbsp coarse grain salt (decrease according to taste, see page 25)
- 3 tbsp neutral-tasting oil, plus more for greasing the tin
- 50g/2oz oat bran
- 40g/1½oz wheat bran
- 130g/4½oz rolled oats
- 70g/2½oz wholemeal flour
- 595g/1lb 5oz unbleached plain flour

1. Mixing and storing the dough: mix the yeast and salt with the water, milk, maple syrup and oil in a 5 litre/8¾ pint bowl, or a lidded (not airtight) food container.

2. Mix in the remaining dry ingredients without kneading, using a spoon, a 3.5 litre/6 pint-capacity food processor (with dough attachment), or a heavy-duty stand mixer (with dough hook). If you're not using a machine, you may need to use wet hands to incorporate the last bit of flour.

3. Cover (not airtight), and allow to rest at room temperature until the dough rises and collapses (or flattens on top), approximately 2 hours.

4. The dough can be used immediately after the initial rise, though it is easier to handle when cold. Refrigerate in a lidded (not airtight) container and use over the next 8 days.

5. On baking day, lightly grease a 23 x 10 x 7.5cm/9 x 4 x 3in non-stick loaf tin. Dust the surface of the refrigerated dough with flour and cut off a 675g/1½lb (cantaloupe-size) piece. Dust the piece with more flour and quickly shape it into a ball by stretching the surface of the dough around to the bottom on all four sides, rotating the ball a quarter turn as you go.

6. Elongate the ball into an oval and place it into the prepared tin. Allow to rest and rise for 1 hour and 20 minutes (or just 40 minutes if you're using fresh, unrefrigerated dough).

7. Thirty minutes before baking time, preheat the oven to 190°C/gas mark 5, with an empty grill tray on any other shelf that won't interfere with the rising bread. If you're not using a stone, the preheat can be as short as 5 minutes.

8. Place the loaf on a rack near the centre of the oven. Pour 250ml/8 fl oz of hot tap water into the grill tray and quickly close the oven door. Bake for 45 to 50 minutes, or until deeply browned and firm.

9. Allow to cool before slicing or eating.

Laura's Three-Citrus Marmalade

Here's something sweet yet startlingly tart to put on your Oatmeal Bread (see page 112), or just about anything else. Citrus fruits can be had all year but, if you wait until the height of the season, the selection increases. Try substituting blood oranges or tangerines for the navel oranges when in season.

'My wife, Laura, does the jam making in our house, and she makes a marmalade that everyone loves. I wish I could say that the recipe was whispered to her in an Italian citrus grove, but Laura enjoys telling foodies that it comes from the instruction sheet inside the pectin box. But she is too modest. Laura adapted the original recipe by adding pink grapefruit, which brings a touch of extra tartness that makes the marmalade unique.'
– Jeff

Makes 1.8kg/4 lb.

- 4 navel oranges
- 1 lemon
- ½ pink grapefruit
- 600ml/1 pint water
- ⅛ tsp bicarbonate of soda
- 1.1kg/2lb 6oz sugar
- 45g/1¾oz pectin

1. Using a vegetable peeler, remove the coloured zest from the fruit and discard the white pith. Chop the zest coarsely.

2. Chop the fruit, discarding any seeds and reserving the juice.

3. Place the zests, water and bicarbonate of soda into a saucepan and bring to a boil. Reduce heat; cover and simmer 20 minutes, stirring occasionally. Add fruit and juice; simmer another 10 minutes.

4. Measure the sugar and set aside. Do not reduce the sugar, or marmalade may not set properly.

5. Stir the pectin into the fruit mixture. Bring to a full, rolling boil.

6. Stir in the sugar quickly, return to a full rolling boil, and cook for 1 minute. Remove from the heat and skim off any foam.

7. Pour the hot marmalade into clean sterilised jars (see box opposite) place a waxed disc over the surface, then seal with a lid. Store the jars in a cool dry place.

To sterilise glass jars

You can use the method below, but to be sure you sterilise the jars effectively, please follow the manufacturer's instructions.

Preheat the oven to 120°C/gas mark ½.

If you have a dishwasher, put the jars and lids in and wash them on a high temperature – this should be enough to sterilise the jars. Then put the jars in the oven for 15 minutes to dry them out.

If you don't have a dishwasher, wash the jars in hot soapy water, rinse and then put them in an oven which has been preheated to 200°C/gas mark 6 for 15 minutes. Do this while you are cooking so they are hot enough that they won't crack when you pour in the hot marmalade.

Sterilize the jar lids by placing them in boiling water whilst the jars are in the oven.

Raisin-Walnut Oatmeal Bread

Full of the flavours we associate with oatmeal – raisins, walnuts and a touch of maple syrup, this reminds us of the breakfasts our mothers made when we were kids. And now it will be the breakfast your kids beg you to make.

Makes 1 loaf.

- Neutral-tasting oil for greasing the tin
- 675g/1½lb (cantaloupe-size portion) Oatmeal Bread dough (page 112)
- 175g/6oz raisins
- 75g/3oz walnuts
- Egg wash (1 egg beaten with 1 tbsp of water)

Variation:
Substitute 175g/6oz chopped dried apricots for the raisins.

1. On baking day, lightly grease a 23 x 10 x 7.5cm/9 x 4 x 3in non-stick loaf tin. Dust the surface of the refrigerated dough with flour and cut off a 675g/1½lb (cantaloupe-size) piece. Dust the piece with more flour and quickly shape it into a ball by stretching the surface of the dough around to the bottom on all four sides, rotating the ball a quarter turn as you go.

2. Flatten the dough with your hands and roll out into a 1cm/½in-thick rectangle. As you roll out the dough, use enough flour to prevent it from sticking to the work surface but not so much as to make the dough dry.

3. Sprinkle the raisins and walnuts over the dough and roll the dough up to encase them. Fold the dough over again and then shape to approximate a loaf shape, using a small amount of flour if necessary.

4. Place the loaf in the prepared tin, and allow to rest for approximately 1 hour and 40 minutes (or just 40 minutes if you're using fresh, unrefrigerated dough).

5. Thirty minutes before baking time, preheat the oven to 190°C/gas mark 5. If you're not using a stone, the preheat can be as short as 5 minutes. Brush the loaf with the egg wash. Bake for approximately 45 minutes or until golden brown.

6. Allow to cool before slicing or eating.

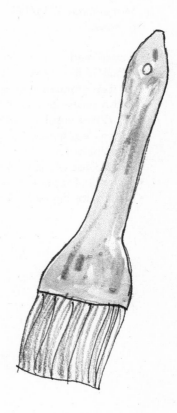

Oatmeal Pumpkin Bread

Roasting the pumpkin caramelises the sugars and intensifies the flavours, so it's worth the effort to do your own rather than substituting with canned pumpkin purée in this bread. Be sure to choose a smaller pumpkin and not the watery and flavourless decorative pumpkin.

'In the autumn at my house, there is almost always a pumpkin roasting for pie and a batch of oatmeal cooking for breakfast. This is Minnesota and these are the things that keep us warm and happy. One day I had both going, and decided to try combining them into a bread. Well, it worked beautifully and is now one of my family's favourites. For obvious reasons I tend to make a lot of it right around Thanksgiving. It's perfect with left-over turkey.' – Zoë

Makes three 675g/1½lb loaves. The recipe is easily doubled or halved.

- 1 small-medium pumpkin
- 475ml/16 fl oz lukewarm water
- 1½ tbsp granulated yeast (decrease according to taste, see page 23)
- 1 tbsp coarse grain salt (decrease according to taste, see page 25)
- 65g/2½oz unsalted butter, melted
- 5 tbsp clear honey
- 50g/2oz oats
- 105g/3¾oz wholemeal flour
- 560g/1lb 4oz unbleached plain flour
- Neutral-tasting oil for greasing the tin

1. Preheat the oven to 190°C/gas mark 5. Split the pumpkin in half starting at the stem and place cut side down on a silicone mat or a lightly greased baking sheet. Bake for 45 minutes. The pumpkin should be very soft all the way through when poked with a knife. Cool slightly before scooping out the seeds.

2. Scoop out the roasted flesh of the pumpkin and mash it with a fork or purée it in the food processor. You need 225g/8oz of purée for the dough.

3. Mixing and storing the dough: mix the yeast and salt with the water, melted butter and honey in a 5 litre/8¾ pint bowl, or a lidded (not airtight) food container.

4. Mix in the oats, pumpkin and flours without kneading, using a spoon, a 3.5 litre/6 pint-capacity food processor (with dough attachment), or a heavy-duty stand mixer (with dough hook). If you're not using a machine, you may need to use wet hands to incorporate the last bit of flour.

5. Cover (not airtight), and allow to rest at room temperature until the dough rises and collapses (or flattens on top), approximately 2 hours.

6. The dough can be used immediately after the initial rise, though it is easier to handle when cold. Refrigerate in a lidded (not airtight) container and use over the next 9 days.

7. On baking day, lightly grease a 23 x 13 x 7.5cm/9 x 5 x 3in non-stick loaf tin. Dust the surface of the refrigerated dough with flour and cut off a 675g/1½lb (cantaloupe-size) piece. Dust the piece with more flour and quickly shape it into a ball by stretching the surface of the dough around to the bottom on all four sides, rotating the ball a quarter turn as you go.

8. Place the dough in the prepared tin, and allow to rest and rise for 2 hours (or just 40 minutes if you're using fresh, unrefrigerated dough).

9. Thirty minutes before baking time, preheat the oven to 190°C/gas mark 5, with an empty grill tray for water on any other shelf that won't interfere with the rising bread. If you're not using a stone, the preheat can be as short as 5 minutes.

10. Place the loaf on a rack near the centre of the oven. Pour 250ml/8 fl oz of hot tap water into the grill tray and quickly close the oven door. Bake for 45 to 50 minutes, or until deeply browned and firm.

11. Allow to cool before slicing or eating.

Oatmeal Pumpkin Seed Bread

To jazz up the Oatmeal Pumpkin Bread (page 118), roll in pumpkin seeds and dried cranberries. It adds both a sweet element and a tartness that is wonderful with the other flavours. You can buy ready-toasted pumpkin seeds in supermarkets.

Makes 1 loaf.

- Neutral-tasting oil for greasing the tin
- 675g/1½lb (cantaloupe-size portion) Oatmeal Pumpkin dough (page 118)
- 25g/1oz toasted pumpkin seeds
- 50g/2oz dried cranberries
- Egg wash (one egg beaten with 1 tbsp of water)

1. On baking day, lightly grease a 23 x 10 x 7.5cm/9 x 4 x 3in non-stick loaf tin. Dust the surface of the refrigerated dough with flour and cut off a 675g/1½lb (grapefruit-size) piece. Dust the piece with more flour and quickly shape it into a ball by stretching the surface of the dough around to the bottom on all four sides, rotating the ball a quarter turn as you go.

2. Flatten the dough with your hands and roll out into a 1cm/½in-thick rectangle. As you roll out the dough, use enough flour to prevent it from sticking to the work surface but not so much as to make the dough dry.

3. Sprinkle the seeds and cranberries over the dough and roll the dough up to encase them. Fold the dough over again to work the seeds into the dough.

4. Using a small amount of flour, form the dough into a loaf shape. Place the loaf in the prepared pan and allow to rest and rise 2 hours (or just 40 minutes if you're using fresh, unrefrigerated dough).

5. Thirty minutes before baking time, preheat the oven to 190°C/gas mark 5, and place an empty grill tray on any other shelf that won't interfere with the rising bread. The baking stone is not essential for loaf-tin breads; if you omit it, the preheat may be as short as 5 minutes.

6. Just before putting the bread in the oven, brush the loaf with egg wash and place it on a rack near the centre of the oven. Pour 250ml/8 fl oz of hot tap water into the grill tray and quickly close the oven door. Bake the loaf for 45 to 50 minutes, until deeply browned and firm.

7. Allow to cool before slicing or eating.

Oat Flour Bread

If you're looking for a delicious and sneaky way to get kids to eat more fibre, here is a very simple recipe with a milder taste than most whole grains. Oat flour has more soluble fibre than wholemeal flour.

Makes three 675g/1½lb loaves. The recipe is easily doubled or halved.

- 800ml/27 fl oz lukewarm water
- 1½ tbsp granulated yeast (decrease according to taste, see page 23)
- 1½ tbsp coarse grain salt (decrease according to taste, see page 25)
- 140g/5oz oat flour
- 770g/1lb 11oz unbleached plain flour
- Neutral-tasting oil for greasing the tin

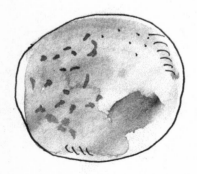

1. Mixing and storing the dough: mix the yeast and salt with the water in a 5 litre/8¾ pint bowl, or a lidded (not airtight) food container.

2. Mix in the flours without kneading, using a spoon, a 3.5 litre/6 pint-capacity food processor (with dough attachment), or a heavy-duty stand mixer (with dough hook). If you're not using a machine, you may need to use wet hands to incorporate the last bit of flour.

3. Cover (not airtight), and allow to rest at room temperature until the dough rises and collapses (or flattens on top), approximately 2 hours.

4. The dough can be used immediately after the initial rise, though it is easier to handle when cold. Refrigerate in a lidded (not airtight) container and use over the next 10 days.

5. On baking day, lightly grease a 23 x 13 x 7.5cm/9 x 5 x 3in non-stick loaf tin. Dust the surface of the refrigerated dough with flour and cut off a 675g/1½lb (cantaloupe-size) piece. Dust the piece with more flour and quickly shape it into a ball by stretching the surface of the dough around to the bottom on all four sides, rotating the ball a quarter turn as you go. Drop into the prepared tin. Allow to rest and rise for 1 hour and 40 minutes (or just 40 minutes if you're using fresh, unrefrigerated dough).

6. Thirty minutes before baking time, preheat the oven to 200°C/gas mark 6, with an empty grill tray on any other shelf that won't interfere with the rising bread. The baking stone is not essential for loaf-tin breads; if you omit it, the preheat may be as short as 5 minutes.

7. Place the loaf on a rack near the centre of the oven. Pour 250ml/8 fl oz of hot tap water into the grill tray and quickly close the oven door. Bake for 45 minutes, or until deeply browned and firm. Smaller or larger loaves will require adjustments in baking time.

8. Allow to cool before slicing or eating.

Vermont Cheddar Bread

Great cheese bread is a wonderful American speciality, and a complete meal in a slice. The success of this loaf will depend on the cheese you use, so go with a great one.

'I grew up in Vermont, where eating sharp, aged cheddar is a birthright. Every Vermont bakery offers its own version of cheddar bread, using cheese from local dairies. Substitute your favourite cheddar or other sharp-flavoured hard cheese in this delicious bread.' – **Zoë**

Makes four 450g/1lb loaves. The recipe is easily doubled or halved.

- 750ml/1¼ pints lukewarm water
- 1½ tbsp granulated yeast (decrease according to taste, see page 23)
- 1½ tbsp coarse grain salt (decrease according to taste, see page 25)
- 1½ tbsp sugar
- 900g/2lb unbleached plain flour
- 115g/4oz cheddar cheese, grated
- Polenta or parchment paper for pizza peel, see page 29

1. Mixing and storing the dough: mix the yeast, salt and sugar with the water in a 5 litre/8¾ pint bowl, or a lidded (not airtight) food container.

2. Mix in the dry ingredients and the cheese without kneading, using a spoon, a 3.5 litre/6 pint-capacity food processor (with dough attachment), or a heavy-duty stand mixer (with dough hook). If you're not using a machine, you may need to use wet hands to incorporate the last bit of flour.

3. Cover (not airtight), and allow to rest at room temperature until the dough rises and collapses (or flattens on top), approximately 2 hours.

4. The dough can be used immediately after the initial rise, though it is easier to handle when cold. Refrigerate in a lidded (not airtight) container and use over the next 7 days.

5. On baking day, dust the surface of the refrigerated dough with flour and cut off a 450g/1lb (grapefruit-size) piece. Dust the piece with more flour and quickly shape it into a ball by stretching the surface of the dough around to the bottom on all four sides, rotating the ball a quarter turn as you go. Allow to rest and rise on a polenta-covered pizza peel for 1 hour (or just 40 minutes if you're using fresh, unrefrigerated dough).

6. Thirty minutes before baking time, preheat the oven to 230°C/gas mark 8, with a baking stone placed on the lowest rack (consider a longer preheat if you're finding your results to be denser than you like, see page 34). Place an empty grill tray on any other shelf that won't interfere with the rising bread.

7. Sprinkle the loaf liberally with flour and slash a deep cross, scallop or criss-cross pattern into the top, using a serrated bread knife. Leave the flour in place for baking; tap some of it off before eating.

8. Slide the loaf directly onto the hot stone. Pour 250ml/8 fl oz of hot tap water into the grill tray, and quickly close the oven door. Bake for about 25 minutes, or until deeply browned and firm. Smaller or larger loaves will require adjustments in baking time.

9. Allow to cool before slicing or eating.

Caramelised Onion and Herb Dinner Rolls

'A friend once told me she times her cooking so that the onions are caramelising as her guests arrive, claiming there is nothing more aromatic and inviting. I can't help but agree with her.' – Zoë

Caramelising the onions is easy and rewarding and can be used to dress up any of our savoury doughs. Another favourite is to use the onion mixture with Manchego cheese as a pizza topping (page 153). Because it takes some time to achieve perfectly caramelised onions you may want to double the recipe to have some on hand; they freeze for months.

Makes 6 dinner rolls.

Use any of these refrigerated pre-mixed doughs: Boule (page 44), Vermont Cheddar (page 124), or European Peasant (page 66).

- 450g/1lb (grapefruit-size portion) of any pre-mixed dough listed above
- 3 tbsp olive oil
- 2 large onions, chopped
- 1 tsp salt (decrease according to taste, see page 25)
- 1 tbsp vermouth or white wine
- 1 tsp white wine vinegar
- 2 tbsp brown sugar
- 1 tsp dried thyme or oregano or 2 tsp chopped fresh thyme and oregano leaves
- 4 tbsp water
- Freshly ground black pepper to taste
- Polenta or parchment paper for pizza peel, see page 29

1. Heat the olive oil in a large frying pan on medium-low heat. Add the onions, salt, vermouth, vinegar, brown sugar, herbs and water to the oil and cook for about 25 minutes, stirring occasionally, until the onions are nicely caramelised. Add more water when needed to prevent burning.

2. Dust the surface of the refrigerated dough with flour and cut off a 450g/1lb (grapefruit-size) piece. Dust the piece with more flour and quickly shape it into a ball by stretching the surface of the dough around to the bottom on all four sides, rotating the ball a quarter turn as you go.

3. To form the dinner rolls, divide the ball into 6 roughly equal portions (each about the size of a plum). Shape each one into a smooth ball. Allow them to rest and rise on a polenta-covered pizza peel for 40 minutes (or just 20 minutes if you're using fresh, unrefrigerated dough). Consider a longer rest time if you're finding your results to be denser than you like, see page 39.

4. Thirty minutes before baking time, preheat the oven to 230°C/gas mark 8, with a baking stone placed on the middle rack (consider a longer preheat if you're finding your results to be denser than you like, see page 34). Place an empty grill tray on any other shelf that won't interfere with the rising bread.

5. Just before baking, sprinkle the rolls liberally with flour and cut a 1cm/½in cross pattern into the top, using a serrated bread knife or sharp kitchen scissors. Fill the resulting space with about 1 tablespoon of the onion mixture.

6. Slide the rolls directly onto the hot stone. Pour 250ml/8 fl oz of hot tap water into the grill tray, and quickly close the oven door. Bake for 20 to 25 minutes, or until deeply browned and firm.

7. Allow to cool before eating.

Spinach Feta Bread

Spinach and feta cheese are usually seen wrapped in flaky filo pastry dough as savoury Greek spinach pies. Our bread version is hearty, satisfying and much easier to make. Serve with Greek olives for a fantastic and easy appetiser.

Makes four 450g/1lb loaves. The recipe is easily doubled or halved.

- 115g/4oz cooked (lightly steamed, boiled or sautéed), chopped spinach
- 750ml/1¼ pints lukewarm water
- 1½ tbsp granulated yeast (decrease according to taste, see page 23)
- 1 tbsp coarse grain salt (decrease according to taste, see page 25)
- 40g/1½oz crumbled feta cheese
- 1½ tbsp sugar
- 900g/2lb plain flour
- Polenta or parchment paper for pizza peel, see page 29

1. Mixing and storing the dough: squeeze the cooked spinach through a sieve to get rid of excess liquid.

2. Mix the yeast, salt, spinach, cheese and sugar with the water in a 5 litre/8¾ pint bowl, or a lidded (not airtight) food container.

3. Mix in the flour without kneading, using a spoon, a 3.5 litre/6 pint-capacity food processor (with dough attachment), or a heavy-duty stand mixer (with dough hook). If you're not using a machine, you may need to use wet hands to incorporate the last bit of flour.

4. Cover (not airtight), and allow to rest at room temperature until the dough rises and collapses (or flattens on top), approximately 2 hours.

5. The dough can be used immediately after the initial rise, though it is easier to handle when cold. Refrigerate in a lidded (not airtight) container and use over the next 7 days.

6. On baking day, dust the surface of the refrigerated dough with flour and cut off a 450g/1lb (grapefruit-size) piece. Dust the piece with more flour and quickly shape it into a ball by stretching the surface of the dough around to the bottom on all four sides, rotating the ball a quarter turn as you go. Allow to rest and rise on a polenta-covered pizza peel for 1 hour (or just 40 minutes if you're using fresh, unrefrigerated dough).

7. Thirty minutes before baking time, preheat the oven to 230°C/gas mark 8, with a baking stone placed on the middle rack (consider a longer preheat if you're finding your results to be denser than you like, see page 34). Place an empty grill tray on any other shelf that won't interfere with the rising bread.

8. Sprinkle the loaf liberally with flour and slash a deep cross, scallop or criss-cross pattern into the top, using a serrated bread knife. Leave the flour in place for baking; tap some of it off before eating.

9. Slide the loaf directly onto the hot stone. Pour 250ml/8 fl oz of hot tap water into the grill tray, and quickly close the oven door. Bake for 30 to 35 minutes, or until deeply browned and firm. Smaller or larger loaves will require adjustments in baking time.

10. Allow to cool before slicing or eating.

Sun-Dried Tomato and Parmesan Bread

Bright and intense tomato flavours harmonise nicely with the richness of aged Italian cheese. That's a combination we love in pasta dishes, so we created a bread with those flavours. If you can get authentic Parmigiano Reggiano, use it here; if not, use whatever hard Italian grating cheese you like on your pasta.

Makes 1 loaf.

Use any of these refrigerated pre-mixed doughs: Boule (page 44), European Peasant (page 66), Olive Oil (page 150), Light Wholemeal (page 94), or Italian Semolina (page 100).

- 450g/1lb (grapefruit-size portion) of any pre-mixed dough listed above
- Olive oil for brushing the loaf
- 50g/2oz sun-dried tomatoes in oil, drained and roughly chopped
- 40g/1½oz grated Parmigiano Reggiano cheese
- Polenta or parchment paper for pizza peel, see page 29

1. On baking day, dust the surface of the refrigerated dough with flour and cut off a 450g/1lb (grapefruit-size) piece. Dust the piece with more flour and quickly shape it into a ball by stretching the surface of the dough around to the bottom on all four sides, rotating the ball a quarter turn as you go.

2. Roll out the ball into a 5mm/¼in-thick rectangle. As you roll out the dough, use enough flour to prevent it from sticking to the work surface but not so much as to make the dough dry.

3. Brush the dough with olive oil. Scatter the sun-dried tomatoes evenly over the dough and sprinkle the cheese over the tomatoes. Starting from the short end, roll the dough into a log and gently tuck the ends under to form an oval loaf. Allow to rest and rise on a polenta-covered pizza peel for 1 hour (or just 40 minutes if you're using fresh, unrefrigerated dough).

4. Thirty minutes before baking time, preheat the oven to 230°C/gas mark 8, with a baking stone placed on the middle rack (consider a longer preheat if you're finding your results to be denser than you like, see page 34). Place an empty grill tray on any other shelf that won't interfere with the rising bread.

5. Brush the top of the dough lightly with olive oil and slash parallel cuts across the loaf, using a serrated bread knife.

6. Slide the loaf directly onto the hot stone. Pour 250ml/8 fl oz of hot tap water into the grill tray, and quickly close the oven door. Bake for 30 to 35 minutes, or until deeply browned and firm.

7. Allow to cool before slicing or eating.

Aunt Melissa's Muesli Bread

The key to great muesli bread, is – surprise – great homemade muesli (page 134). You can use packaged muesli but it won't have quite the same flavour. Make lots of your own and there'll be plenty left over for breakfast.

'As a small child, I lived on a commune in the North East Kingdom of Vermont with my dad and my Aunt Melissa, where they made muesli and bread to sell at the local co-op. My main contribution was to eat great quantities of the muesli. I still remember the sweet earthy smell of the house when Melissa would bake. Aunt Melissa has since passed away, and with her went the original recipe, but this is a very close approximation.' – Zoë

Makes two 675g/1½lb loaves. The recipe is easily doubled or halved.

- 475ml/16 fl oz lukewarm water
- 1½ tbsp granulated yeast
- 8 tbsp clear honey
- 1 tbsp neutral-flavoured oil
- 1 tsp ground cinnamon
- 1 tbsp coarse grain salt (decrease according to taste, see page 25)
- 210g/7½oz wholemeal flour
- 350g/12oz unbleached plain flour
- 175g/6oz muesli, plus a few tbsp to sprinkle on top (see page 134 for Home-Made Muesli)
- Neutral-tasting oil for greasing the tin
- Egg wash (1 egg beaten with 1 tbsp of water)

1. Mixing and storing the dough: mix the yeast, honey, oil, cinnamon and salt with the water in a 5 litre/8¾ pint bowl, or a lidded (not airtight) food container.

2. Mix in the flours and muesli without kneading, using a spoon, a 3.5 litre/6 pint-capacity food processor (with dough attachment), or a heavy-duty stand mixer (with dough hook). If you're not using a machine, you may need to use wet hands to incorporate the last bit of flour.

3. Cover (not airtight), and allow to rest at room temperature until the dough rises and collapses (or flattens on top), approximately 2 hours.

4. The dough can be used immediately after the initial rise, though it is easier to handle when cold. Refrigerate in a lidded (not airtight) container and use over the next 5 days.

5. On baking day, grease a 23 x 10 x 7.5cm/ 9 x 4 x 3in non-stick loaf tin. Dust the surface of the refrigerated dough with flour and cut off a 675g/1½lb (grapefruit-size) piece. Dust the piece with more flour and quickly shape it into a ball by stretching the surface of the dough around to the bottom on all four sides, rotating the ball a quarter turn as you go. Drop into the prepared tin. Allow to rest and rise for 1 hour and 40 minutes (or just 1 hour if you're using fresh, unrefrigerated dough).

6. Thirty minutes before baking time, preheat the oven to 190°C/gas mark 5). If you're not using a stone, the preheat can be as short as 5 minutes.

7. Place the bread in the centre of the oven and bake for about 45 minutes, or until richly browned and firm.

8. Allow to cool before slicing or eating.

Home-Made Muesli for Muesli Bread

Use this muesli in Aunt Melissa's Muesli Bread, or enjoy it with milk for breakfast.

Makes about 675g/1½ lb.

- 6 tbsp clear honey
- 3 tbsp maple syrup
- 5 tbsp neutral-flavoured oil
- 2 tbsp water
- ½ tsp vanilla extract
- ¼ tsp ground cinnamon
- ¼ tsp salt (decrease according to taste, see page 25)
- 350g/12oz rolled oats
- 50g/2oz sesame seeds
- 75g/3oz chopped pecans or the nut of your choice
- 65g/2½oz desiccated coconut
- 75g/3oz raisins
- 115g/4oz dried cherries, chopped dried apricots or dried cranberries (or a combination)

1. Preheat the oven to 190°C/gas mark 5. Prepare a baking tray with parchment paper, oil, butter, or a large silicone mat.

2. Mix honey, maple syrup, oil, water, vanilla extract, cinnamon and salt in a measuring jug.

3. In a large bowl, combine the liquid mixture with the dry ingredients, except for the dried fruit, and mix until everything is coated with the honey mixture. Spread the mixture evenly over the prepared baking tray. Bake for about 30 minutes, stirring every 10 minutes, until the muesli is golden brown. Baking time will vary, depending on the depth of muesli on the baking tray.

4. After the baking is complete, add the dried fruit.

5. Allow to cool, store in jars and use in Aunt Melissa's Muesli Bread (page 132).

Roasted Garlic Potato Bread

Skin on and roughly mashed is the way we prefer our potatoes, but if you want yours peeled and perfectly puréed that will work as well. The roasted garlic is sweet and pungent; this bread explodes with aroma when you break into it.

Makes four 450g/1lb loaves. The recipe is easily doubled or halved.

- 1 whole head of garlic
- 750ml/1¼ pints lukewarm water
- 1½ tbsp granulated yeast (decrease according to taste, see page 23)
- 1½ tbsp coarse grain salt (decrease according to taste, see page 25)
- 1½ tbsp sugar
- 75g/3oz mashed potato
- 900g/2lb unbleached plain flour
- Polenta or parchment paper for pizza peel, see page 29

1. Roast a whole head of garlic by wrapping it in foil and baking for 30 minutes at 200°C/gas mark 6. Allow to cool and cut off the top of the head. Squeeze out the roasted garlic, measure 2 tablespoons and set aside.

2. Mixing and storing the dough: mix the yeast, salt, sugar, mashed potato and reserved roasted garlic with the water in a 5 litre/8¾ pint bowl, or a lidded (not airtight) food container.

3. Mix in the flour without kneading, using a spoon, a 3.5 litre/6 pint-capacity food processor (with dough attachment), or a heavy-duty stand mixer (with dough hook). If you're not using a machine, you may need to use wet hands to incorporate the last bit of flour.

4. Cover (not airtight), and allow to rest at room temperature until the dough rises and collapses (or flattens on top), approximately 2 hours.

5. The dough can be used immediately after the initial rise, though it is easier to handle when cold. Refrigerate in a lidded (not airtight) container and use over the next 7 days.

6. On baking day, dust the surface of the refrigerated dough with flour and cut off a 450g/1lb (grapefruit-size) piece. Dust the piece with more flour and quickly shape it into a ball by stretching the surface of the dough around to the bottom on all four sides, rotating the ball a quarter turn as you go. Allow to rest and rise on a polenta-covered pizza peel for 1 hour (or just 40 minutes if you're using fresh, unrefrigerated dough).

7. Thirty minutes before baking time, preheat the oven to 230°C/gas mark 8, with a baking stone placed on the middle rack of the oven (consider a longer preheat if you're finding your results to be denser than you like, see page 34). Place a grill tray for water on any other shelf that won't interfere with the rising bread.

8. Sprinkle the loaf liberally with flour and slash a deep cross, scallop or criss-cross pattern into the top, using a serrated bread knife. Leave the flour in place for baking; tap some of it off before eating.

9. Slide the loaf directly onto the hot stone. Pour 250ml/8 fl oz of hot tap water into the grill tray, and quickly close the oven door. Bake for 30 to 35 minutes, or until deeply browned and firm. Smaller or larger loaves will require adjustments in baking time.

10. Allow to cool before slicing or eating.

Eastern European Potato Rye Bread

Here's another potato bread, with a difference. Hold the roasted garlic and bring on the caraway seeds. This one's a very moist and rustic Eastern European masterpiece. The bread will still be fresh the day after baking because the potato and rye hold moisture and prevent it from drying out.

Makes four 450g/1lb loaves. The recipe is easily doubled or halved.

- 750ml/1¼ pints lukewarm water
- 1½ tbsp granulated yeast (decrease according to taste, see page 23)
- 1½ tbsp coarse grain salt (decrease according to taste, see page 25)
- 75g/3oz mashed potato
- 1½ tbsp caraway seeds, plus additional for sprinkling on the top crust
- 140g/5oz rye flour
- 770g/1lb 11oz unbleached plain flour
- Polenta or parchment paper for pizza peel, see page 29
- Cornflour wash (see box, page 73)

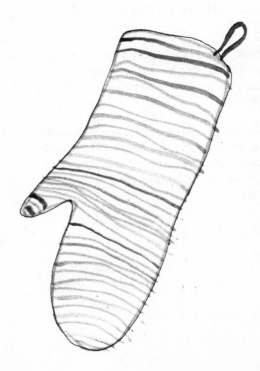

1. Mixing and storing the dough: mix the yeast, salt, mashed potato and caraway seeds with the water in a 5 litre/8¾ pint bowl, or a lidded (not airtight) food container.

2. Mix in the rye and plain flour without kneading, using a spoon, a 3.5 litre/6 pint-capacity food processor (with dough attachment), or a heavy-duty stand mixer (with dough hook). If you're not using a machine, you may need to use wet hands to incorporate the last bit of flour.

3. Cover (not airtight), and allow to rest at room temperature until the dough rises and collapses (or flattens on top), approximately 2 hours.

4. The dough can be used immediately after the initial rise, though it is easier to handle when cold. Refrigerate in a lidded (not airtight) container and use over the next 9 days.

5. On baking day, dust the surface of the refrigerated dough with flour and cut off a 450g/1lb (grapefruit-size) piece. Dust the piece with more flour and quickly shape it into a ball by stretching the surface of the dough around to the bottom on all four sides, rotating the ball a quarter turn as you go. Allow to rest and rise on a polenta-covered pizza peel for 1 hour (or just 40 minutes if you're using fresh, unrefrigerated dough).

6. Thirty minutes before baking time, preheat the oven to 230°C/gas mark 8, with a baking stone placed on the middle rack (consider a longer preheat if you're finding your results to be denser than you like, see page 34). Place an empty grill tray on any other shelf that won't interfere with the rising bread.

7. Using a pastry brush, paint the top crust with cornflour wash and then sprinkle with the additional caraway seeds. Slash the loaf with deep parallel cuts across the loaf; the cornflour wash should allow the knife to pass without sticking.

8. Slide the loaf directly onto the hot stone. Pour 250ml/8 fl oz of hot tap water into the grill tray, and quickly close the oven door. Bake for 30 to 35 minutes, until deeply browned and firm. Smaller or larger loaves will require adjustments in baking time.

9. Allow to cool before slicing or eating.

Bagels

These bagels are lighter than typical American-style bagels because we let them rest briefly while the oven is heating up, rather than boiling them immediately after shaping. They can be made the traditional way (forming and immediately boiling) for a denser result. This dough stores as well as any of our other recipes and can be used for soft pretzels (page 144), bialys (page 142) or even free-form loaves.

Makes about 20 bagels. The recipe is easily doubled or halved.

The Dough
- 750ml/1¼ pints lukewarm water
- 1½ tbsp granulated yeast (decrease according to taste, see page 23)
- 1½ tbsp coarse grain salt (decrease according to taste, see page 25)
- 1½ tbsp sugar
- 875g/1lb 15oz strong flour

The Boiling Pot
- 8 litres/14 pints boiling water
- 50g/2oz sugar
- 1 tsp bicarbonate of soda
- Poppy or sesame seeds
- Extra flour for dusting towel
- Wholemeal flour or parchment paper for pizza peel, see page 29

1. Mixing and storing the bagel dough: mix the yeast, salt and sugar with the water in a 5 litre/8¾ pint bowl, or a lidded (not airtight) food container.

2. Mix in the flour without kneading, using a spoon, a 3.5 litre/6 pint-capacity food processor (with dough attachment), or a heavy-duty stand mixer (with dough hook). If you're not using a machine, you may need to use wet hands to incorporate the last bit of flour.

3. Cover (not airtight), and allow to rest at room temperature until the dough rises and collapses (or flattens on top), approximately 2 hours.

4. The dough can be used immediately after the initial rise, though it is easier to handle when cold. Refrigerate in a lidded (not airtight) container and use over the next 14 days.

Forming, Boiling and Baking the Bagels

5. Thirty minutes before baking time, preheat the oven to 230°C/gas mark 8, with a baking stone placed near the middle (consider a longer preheat if you're finding your results to be denser than you like, see page 34). Place an empty grill tray on any other shelf that won't interfere with the rising bagels.

6. Dust the surface of the refrigerated dough with flour and cut off a 75g/3oz piece of dough (about the size of a small peach). Dust the piece with more flour and quickly shape it into a ball by stretching the surface of the dough around to the bottom on all four sides, rotating the ball a quarter turn as you go.

7. Repeat to form the rest of the bagels. Cover the balls loosely with clingfilm and allow to rest at room temperature for 20 minutes.

8. Prepare the boiling pot: bring a large saucepan or stockpot full of water to the boil. Reduce to a simmer and add the sugar and bicarbonate of soda.

9. Punch your thumb through the dough to form the hole. Ease it open with your fingers until the hole's diameter is about triple the width of the bagel wall.

10. Drop the bagels into the simmering water one at a time, making sure they are not crowding one another. They need enough room to float without touching or they will be misshapen. Let them simmer for 2 minutes and then flip them over with a slotted spoon to cook the other side. Simmer for another minute.

11. Remove them from the water, using the slotted spoon, and place on a clean kitchen towel that has been lightly dusted with flour. This will absorb some of the excess water from the bagels. Then place them on a peel covered with wholemeal flour. Sprinkle the bagels with poppy or sesame seeds.

12. Slide the bagels directly onto the hot stone. Pour 250ml/8 fl oz of hot tap water into the grill tray, and quickly close the oven door. Bake with steam for about 20 minutes, until deeply browned and firm.

13. Break the usual rule for cooling, and serve these a bit warm – they're fantastic!

Bialys

'Bialys (chewy onion-flavoured rolls) have always been something of an obsession for my mother. When I was a little girl, we'd visit my great aunts in Brighton Beach, Brooklyn, and my mother would always stop to pick up bialys and knishes, two things that couldn't be found anywhere in Vermont. Mom's obsession was in full bloom during a recent trip to New York City with her best friend, Barbara. As they left the ballet at Lincoln Center, my mother decided that late-night bialys would make the evening truly perfect. They jumped onto a bus and headed for Kossar's Bakery in lower Manhattan, one of the world's last great bastions of "bialydom". One can only imagine the sight of two women dressed for the ballet getting out of a bus at midnight in front of Kossar's. Only someone obsessed with fresh bialys would understand. Now my mother can make bialys at home.' – Zoë

Makes about 5 bialys.

- 450g/1lb Bagel dough (page 140)
- 1 tbsp vegetable oil
- ½ onion, finely chopped
- ¾ tsp poppy seeds
- Salt and pepper
- Wholemeal flour or parchment paper for pizza peel, see page 29

1. Dust the surface of the refrigerated dough with flour and cut off a 75g/3oz piece of dough (about the size of a small peach). Dust the piece with more flour and quickly shape it into a ball by stretching the surface of the dough around to the bottom on all four sides, rotating the ball a quarter turn as you go. Press the ball into a 7.5cm/3in disc and let rest on a floured surface for 30 minutes. Repeat with as many bialys as you want to bake.

2. Thirty minutes before baking time, preheat the oven to 230°C/gas mark 8, with a baking stone placed near the middle of the oven (consider a longer preheat if you're finding your results to be denser than you like, see page 34). Place an empty grill tray on any other shelf that won't interfere with the rising bialys.

3. While the dough is resting and the oven is preheating, sauté the onions in the vegetable oil over medium heat, until they are translucent and slightly golden. Don't overbrown at this stage, or they will burn in the oven. Remove from heat and add the poppy seeds, and salt and pepper to taste.

4. Press the centre of each bialy to flatten it, working your way out until there is a 1cm/½in rim of dough that is not pressed flat and the bialy is about 10cm/4in wide. Fill the centre with 1 tablespoon of the onion mixture and press it securely into the bialy dough.

5. Dust a pizza peel with wholemeal flour and put the finished bialys on it. Slide the bialys directly onto the hot stone, making sure they are spaced about 2.5cm/1in apart, so they have room to expand. Pour 250ml/8 fl oz of hot tap water into the grill tray, and quickly close the oven door. Bake for about 12 minutes, until golden brown. Don't overbake the bialys or they will lose their chewy soft texture.

6. Allow to cool slightly before eating.

Soft Pretzels

Pretzels are closely related to bagels, also having their origin in Central Europe. You can make fantastic pretzels using our basic Bagel dough (page 140), twisting it into the pretzel shape, which is a traditional symbol of earth and sun. We love them hot, with mustard.

'Food writer Mimi Sheraton ran a newspaper article on home-made pretzels about 30 years ago, and it stuck in my teenage mind – I was taken by her description of the crusty pretzels baked for her by her Stuttgart hosts. I still have the original clipping from 1978, so we've adapted her recipe here.' – Jeff

Makes about 5 pretzels.

The Dough
- 450g/1lb Bagel dough (page 140)
- Egg wash (1 egg beaten with 1 tbsp of water)
- Coarse grain salt for sprinkling
- Extra flour for dusting kitchen towel
- Wholemeal flour or parchment paper for pizza peel, see page 29

The Boiling Pot
- 8 litres/14 pints boiling water
- 1 tsp bicarbonate of soda
- 1 tbsp cream of tartar

1. Dust the surface of the refrigerated dough with flour and cut off a 75g/3oz piece of dough (about the size of a small peach). Dust the piece with more flour and quickly shape it into a ball by stretching the surface of the dough around to the bottom on all four sides, rotating the ball a quarter turn as you go. Elongate the ball, dusting with additional flour as necessary. Roll it back and forth with your hands on a floured surface to form a long rope approximately 1cm/½in in diameter and 30cm/12in long.

2. Twist into a pretzel shape by first tying a knot, then looping the ends around and joining them back to the loop. Repeat, forming as many pretzels as you want to bake.

3. Thirty minutes before baking time, preheat the oven to 230°C/gas mark 8, with a baking stone placed near the middle of the oven. Place an empty grill tray on any other shelf that won't interfere with the rising pretzels.

4. Keep the pretzels covered loosely with clingfilm as you repeat the process to make the rest. Let the pretzels rest at room temperature for 20 minutes.

5. Prepare the boiling pot: bring a large saucepan or stockpot full of water to the boil. Reduce to a simmer and add the bicarbonate of soda and cream of tartar. Drop the pretzels into the simmering water one at a time, making sure they are not crowding one another. They need enough room to float without touching or they will be misshapen. Let them simmer for 2 minutes and then flip them over with a slotted spoon to cook the other side. Simmer for another minute.

6. Remove them from the water, using the slotted spoon, and place on a clean kitchen towel that has been lightly dusted with flour. This will absorb some of the excess water from the pretzels. Then place them on a peel covered with wholemeal flour. Brush with egg wash and sprinkle with coarse grain salt.

7. Slide the pretzels directly onto the hot stone. Pour 250ml/8 fl oz of hot tap water into the grill tray, and quickly close the oven door. Bake with steam for about 15 minutes, until deeply browned and firm. If you want crisp pretzels, bake 5 to 10 minutes longer.

8. Serve these a bit warm, with a glass of beer.

Montreal Bagels

These differ from American-style bagels by the addition of malt powder and honey, and the fact that the toppings are on both sides. In Montreal, bagels are traditionally baked in a wood-fired oven, which imparts a wonderful smokiness, but the ones made on the baking stone at home are excellent as well. This recipe calls for strong flour to ensure that the bagels are nice and chewy – plain flour makes them too cakey.

'My husband, Graham, grew up in Canada eating Montreal bagels. One of the first things we did as a couple was to visit Montreal. As soon as we arrived, we drove to Fairmont Bagels and got a bag of fresh hot bagels – I was in love. Several years later, after a New Year's Eve party in Montreal, Graham proposed to me while eating our favourite bagels. Now that we live in the Midwest without our beloved bagels, I create my own. They may not be baked in a wood-fired oven but they are close, really close, to what I remember.' – Zoë

Makes about 1 dozen bagels. The recipe is easily doubled or halved.

The Dough
- 350ml/12 fl oz lukewarm water
- 1 tbsp granulated yeast (decrease according to taste, see page 23)
- 2 tsp coarse grain salt (decrease according to taste, see page 25)
- 5 tbsp sugar
- 2 tbsp clear honey
- 1 egg
- 3 tbsp neutral-flavoured oil
- 3 tbsp malt powder
- 595g/1lb 5oz strong flour
- Poppy or sesame seeds
- Wholemeal flour or parchment paper for pizza peel, see page 29

The Boiling Pot
- 4 litres/7 pints water
- 2 tbsp clear honey
- 2 tbsp malt powder

1. Mixing and storing the bagel dough: mix the yeast, salt, sugar, honey, egg, oil and malt powder with the lukewarm water in a 5 litre/8¾ pint bowl, or a lidded (not airtight) food container.

2. Mix in the flour without kneading, using a spoon, a 3.5 litre/6 pint-capacity food processor (with dough attachment), or a heavyduty stand mixer (with dough hook). If you're not using a machine, you may need to use wet hands to incorporate the last bit of flour.

3. Cover (not airtight), and allow to rest at room temperature until the dough rises and collapses (or flattens on top), approximately 2 hours.

4. The dough can be used immediately after the initial rise, though it is easier to handle when cold. Refrigerate in a lidded (not airtight) container and use over the next 10 days.

Forming, Boiling and Baking the Bagels

5. Preheat the oven to 200°C/gas mark 6, with a baking stone near the middle of the oven. Place an empty grill tray on any other shelf that won't interfere with the rising bagels.

6. Dust the surface of the refrigerated dough with flour and cut off a 75g/3oz piece of dough (about the size of a small peach). Dust with more flour and quickly shape it into a ball by stretching the surface of the dough around to the bottom on all four sides, rotating the ball a quarter turn as you go.

7. Repeat to form the rest of the bagels. Cover the balls loosely with clingfilm and allow to rest at room temperature for 20 minutes.

8. Prepare the boiling pot: bring a large saucepan or stockpot full of water to the boil. Reduce to a simmer and add the honey and malt powder.

9. Punch your thumb through the dough to form the hole. Ease it open with your fingers until the hole's diameter is about triple the width of the bagel wall.

10. Drop the bagels into the water one at a time, making sure they are not crowding each other. They need enough room to float without touching or they will be misshapen. Let them simmer for 1 minute and then flip them over with a slotted spoon and cook the other side for 30 seconds.

11. Remove them from the water, using the slotted spoon, and place on a clean kitchen towel that has been lightly dusted with flour. This will absorb some of the excess water from the bagels.

12. Dredge each bagel in poppy or sesame seeds on both sides and place on a pizza peel. If making plain bagels, cover the peel with wholemeal flour. Slide the bagels directly on to the hot stone. Pour 250ml/8 fl oz of hot tap water into the grill tray, and quickly close the oven door. Bake with steam for about 20 minutes, until richly browned and firm.

13. Break the usual rule for cooling and serve these a bit warm.

FLATBREADS AND PIZZAS

Flatbreads from Southern Europe (Italian *focaccia*, French Provençal *fougasse*) have been popular in the USA for years (though not as long as pizza). When they first arrived on the scene, their strong flavours seemed exotic, with their luxurious richness and weight derived from olive oil rather than milk, butter or cream. But their originators would have laughed; these were simple peasant loaves, everyday fare without pretension. These fragrant rounds were born in regions where dairy products and butter were greater luxuries than olive oil.

And the Middle East has been producing leavened but flat breads of all kinds for thousands of years. Most Americans are familiar with puffed pitta flatbread, but the aromatic spice-topped Arab *za'atar* flatbread is uncommon outside the Middle East.

Flatbread is marvellously suited to very fast preparation. Because flatbreads are so thin, the dough will warm to room temperature quickly, which means very short, if any, rise time. Pizza, *lavash* and pitta, among others, need none. And thicker flatbreads like *focaccia* do very well with just 15 to 20 minutes, so preheat the oven while you're shaping them.

Once they've had their brief rest, flatbreads also bake faster, as quickly as five minutes for *lavash* and pitta (pages 182 and 178). So if you've stored some dough, you can have fresh flatbread on the table in about 25 minutes!

Olive Oil Dough

This versatile, rich dough works nicely in pizza, focaccia or olive bread. The fruitier the olive oil, the better the flavour.

Makes four 450g/1lb loaves. The recipe is easily doubled or halved.

- 675ml/22 fl oz lukewarm water
- 1½ tbsp granulated yeast (decrease according to taste, see page 23)
- 1½ tbsp coarse grain salt (decrease according to taste, see page 25)
- 1 tbsp sugar
- 3 tbsp extra virgin olive oil
- 900g/2lb unbleached plain flour

1. Mix the yeast, salt, sugar and olive oil with the water in a 5 litre/8¾ pint bowl, or a lidded (not airtight) food container.

2. Mix in the flour without kneading, using a spoon, a 3.5 litre/6 pint-capacity food processor (with dough attachment), or a heavy-duty stand mixer (with dough hook). If you're not using a machine, you may need to use wet hands to incorporate the last bit of flour.

3. Cover (not airtight), and allow to rest at room temperature until dough rises and collapses (or flattens on top), approximately 2 hours.

4. The dough can be used immediately after the initial rise, though it is easier to handle when cold. Refrigerate in a lidded (not airtight) container and use over the next 12 days.

Neapolitan Pizza with Aubergine and Anchovy

No-one ever seems to tire of pizza, so here's our version. We like crisp, thin-crusted, Neapolitan-style pizza, baked at a very high temperature directly on the stone. In home ovens, the maximum temperature is 250°C/gas mark 9 not 370°C as in Naples! Pizza made this way at home, especially if you can get fresh mozzarella, is unlike anything most of us are used to eating. The secret to Neapolitan pizza is to keep the crust thin, don't overload it with toppings, and bake it very quickly at a high temperature so it doesn't all cook down to a soup. You should be able to appreciate the individual ingredients in the topping when the pizza emerges from the oven. And of course, you can put any toppings you like on this pizza.

Makes 1 medium-size pizza (30–35cm/ 12–4in) to serve 2 to 4.

Use any of these refrigerated pre-mixed doughs: Boule (page 44), European Peasant (page 66), Olive Oil (page 150), Light Wholemeal (page 94), or Italian Semolina (page 100).

- 450g/1lb (grapefruit-size portion) of any premixed dough listed above
- 50g/2oz canned chopped tomatoes, sieved to remove excess liquid or prepared tomato sauce
- ½ small aubergine, sliced into 3mm/⅛in-thick rounds, cut into bite-size pieces and brushed with olive oil
- 4 anchovy fillets, from a can or jar, chopped
- 115g/4oz fresh mozzarella cheese, preferably buffalo milk, sliced
- 1 tbsp grated Parmigiano Reggiano cheese
- Polenta or parchment paper for pizza peel, see page 29

Don't Get Smoked out of House and Home: This recipe calls for an extractor fan because there'll be a lot of smoke from stray polenta on such a hot stone. Make sure the stone is scraped clean before preheating. If you don't have an extractor fan, choose a lower oven temperature (230°C/gas mark 8), and bake about 15 to 20 per cent longer. Another option is to bake the pizza on a gas barbecue (see Gas Barbecue Flatbread Baking, pages 156–7).

1. Thirty minutes before baking time, preheat the oven with a baking stone at 250°C/gas mark 9. Shelf placement is not critical for pizza, and you won't be using steam, so you can omit the grill tray.

2. Prepare and measure all the toppings in advance. The key to a pizza that slides right off the peel is to work quickly – don't let the dough sit on the peel any longer than necessary.

3. Dust the surface of the refrigerated dough with flour and cut off a 450g/1lb (grapefruit-size) piece. Dust the piece with more flour and quickly shape it into a ball by stretching the surface of the dough around to the bottom on all four sides, rotating the ball a quarter turn as you go.

4. Flatten the dough with your hands and a rolling pin on a wooden board to produce a 3mm/⅛in-thick round, dust with flour to keep the dough from sticking to the rolling pin and board. A little sticking to the board can be helpful in overcoming the dough's resistance to stretch, so don't over-use flour, and consider using a dough scraper to 'unstick' the dough from the board. You may also need to let the partially rolled dough sit for a few minutes to 'relax' to allow further rolling. At this point, stretching by hand may help, followed by additional rolling. Place the rolled-out dough onto a liberally polentacovered pizza peel.

5. Distribute the tomatoes over the surface of the dough. Do not cover the dough thickly; the quantity specified will leave some of the dough surface exposed.

6. Scatter the mozzarella over the surface of the dough, then the aubergine, anchovies and Parmigiano Reggiano. No further resting is needed prior to baking.

7. If you have an extractor fan, turn it on now, because some of the polenta on the pizza peel will smoke at this temperature (see box, page 151). Slide the pizza directly onto the stone (it may take a number of back-and-forth shakes to dislodge the pizza). Check after 8 to 10 minutes; at this time, turn the pizza around in the oven if one side is browning faster than the other. It may need up to 5 more minutes in the oven.

8. Allow to cool slightly on a cooling rack before serving, to allow the cheese to set.

Variations

Pizza Margherita: This is the classic Italian pizza, with nothing but mozzarella, tomato and a sprinkling of dried oregano. Drizzle with extra virgin olive oil just before baking for authenticity and flavour. If you have fresh oregano, coarsely chop the leaves and put them on the pizza first. Tomato sauce from a jar makes a quick substitute for canned tomatoes. On the other end of the spectrum, try the recipe with in season fresh tomatoes, drained of seeds and liquid and thinly sliced.

Sausage or Pepperoni Pizza: Layer sliced cooked sausage or pepperoni on top of the cheese in a basic tomato and cheese pizza. Always use pre-cooked sausage or the meat will render too much fat as the pizza bakes, which will make the pizza soggy.

Caramelised Onion and Manchego Cheese Pizza: This is a sophisticated combination of flavours, both sweet and savoury. Top with one quantity of caramelised onions (page 126) covered with 75g/3oz of grated Manchego cheese.

Rustic Wild Mushroom and Potato Pizza Provençal

Herbes de Provence give this rustic creation of Zoë's a luscious flavour that will transport you to the lavender and thyme-scented hillsides of the south of France.

Makes 1 medium-size pizza (30–35cm/12–14in) to serve 2 to 4.

Use any of these refrigerated pre-mixed doughs: Boule (page 44), European Peasant (page 66), Olive Oil (page 150), Light Wholemeal (page 94), or Italian Semolina (page 100).

- 450g/1lb (grapefruit-size portion) of any pre-mixed dough listed above
- 2 small new potatoes, skin on and thinly sliced
- 6 large wild mushrooms such as chanterelles, shiitakes, porcini, portobellos or oyster mushrooms, or button mushrooms if wild are not available, thinly sliced
- 2 tbsp olive oil
- 1 tsp *herbes de Provence*
- Salt and freshly ground black pepper to taste
- 5 sun-dried tomatoes in oil, drained and thinly sliced
- 50g/2oz Parmigiano Reggiano cheese, finely grated
- Polenta or parchment paper for pizza peel, see page 29

1. Preheat a baking stone in the oven for at least 20 minutes at 250°C/gas mark 9. Shelf placement is not critical for pizza, and you won't be using steam, so you can omit the grill tray.

2. Prepare and measure all the toppings in advance. The key to a pizza that slides right off the peel is to work quickly – don't let the dough sit on the peel any longer than necessary.

3. Sauté the potatoes and mushrooms in the olive oil until the potatoes are soft. Season with the *herbes de Provence*, salt and pepper.

4. Dust the surface of the refrigerated dough with flour and cut off a 450g/1lb (grapefruit-size) piece. Dust the piece with more flour and quickly shape it into a ball by stretching the surface of the dough around to the bottom on all four sides, rotating the ball a quarter turn as you go.

5. Flatten the dough with your hands and a rolling pin on a wooden board to produce a 3mm/⅛in-thick round. Dust with flour to keep the dough from sticking to the rolling pin and board. A little sticking to the board can be helpful in overcoming the dough's resistance to stretch, so don't over-use flour, and consider using a dough scraper to 'unstick' the dough from the board. You may also need to let the partially rolled dough sit for a few minutes to 'relax' and to allow further rolling. At this point, stretching by hand may help, followed by additional rolling. Place the rolled-out dough onto a liberally polentacovered pizza peel.

6. Distribute the potatoes, mushrooms, and sun-dried tomatoes over the surface of the dough. Do not cover the dough thickly; the quantity specified will leave some of the dough surface exposed.

7. Sprinkle the cheese over the surface of the dough.

8. If you have an extractor fan, turn it on now, because some of the polenta on the pizza peel will smoke at this temperature (see box, page 151). Slide the pizza directly onto the stone (it may take a number of back-and-forth shakes to dislodge the pizza). Check after 8 to 10 minutes; at this time, turn the pizza around in the oven if one side is browning faster than the other. It may need up to 5 more minutes in the oven.

9. Allow to cool slightly on a cooling rack before serving, to allow the cheese to set.

Gas Barbecue Flatbread Baking

For those hot summer days when you want fresh bread but can't stand the idea of turning on the oven, outdoor gas barbecues are the answer. Gas barbecues with a thermometer and a baking stone can produce wonderful breads. When baking in a barbecue, thinner is better. Flatbreads like pitta, naan, *lavash*, *focaccia* and *fougasse* work wonderfully.

General Procedure for Gas Barbecue Baking

1. Dust the surface of refrigerated flatbread dough with flour and cut off a 450g/1lb (grapefruit-size piece). Dust the piece with more flour and quickly shape it into a ball by stretching the surface of the dough around to the bottom on all four sides, rotating the ball a quarter turn as you go. Form a flattened round loaf or a flatbread from your favourite recipe. Allow to rest and rise on a pizza peel as specified in the recipe.

2. Thirty minutes before baking time, place a baking stone on the gas barbecue. Light the barbecue and manipulate the burner controls to maintain desired temperature as measured by the barbecue's thermometer. If the recipe calls for baking with steam, place a metal cup or pan on the stone, off to one side so as not to interfere with the baking bread. If your barbecue has a second shelf on which you can safely balance a grill tray, use that for steam.

3. Slide the loaf onto the hot stone. Bake for about two-thirds of the recommended time, with steam if that's in the recipe.

4. Using a long-handed spatula, flip the bread over onto its top crust (even if this is pitta bread). Remove the water receptacle if you used one.

5. Continue baking for the last one-third of the baking time, until the crust is firm and browned. If you're making pitta, don't allow much browning.

Spinach and Cheese Calzone

Traditional pizzerias turn out folded cheese 'pies' by using the basic ingredients that appear in pizza. We recommend whole-milk ricotta for a rich and creamy filling. The doubled dough thickness means that you need to bake at a lower oven temperature than used for the flat Neapolitan pizza.

Makes 1 medium-size calzone to serve 2 to 4.

Use any of these refrigerated pre-mixed doughs: Boule (page 44), European Peasant (page 66), Olive Oil (page 150), Light Wholemeal (page 94)or Italian Semolina (page 100).

- 450g/1lb (grapefruit-size portion) of any pre-mixed dough listed above
- 1 large garlic clove, finely chopped
- 1 to 2 tbsp olive oil
- 115g/4oz fresh or thawed and drained frozen spinach leaves
- 1 egg
- 225g/8oz whole-milk ricotta cheese
- ¼ tsp salt (decrease according to taste, see page 25)
- Freshly ground black pepper, to taste
- Wholemeal flour or parchment paper for pizza peel, see page 29

1. Thirty minutes before baking time, preheat the oven to 230°C/gas mark 8, with a baking stone (consider a longer preheat if you're finding your results to be denser than you like, see page 34). Place an empty grill tray on any other shelf that won't interfere with the calzone as it rises.

2. Briefly sauté the garlic in the olive oil until fragrant. Add the spinach and sauté for 2 minutes, until wilted. Drain and squeeze the spinach gently, discarding any liquid that may have accumulated.

3. Beat the egg and blend with the ricotta cheese, salt and pepper in a bowl. Mix the spinach with the cheese.

4. Dust the surface of the refrigerated dough with flour and cut off a 450g/1lb (grapefruit-size) piece. Dust the piece with more flour and quickly shape it into a ball by stretching the surface of the dough around to the bottom on all four sides, rotating the ball a quarter turn as you go.

5. Flatten the dough with your hands and a rolling pin on a wooden board to produce a 3mm/⅛in-thick round, dusting lightly with flour, as needed, to keep the dough from sticking to the rolling pin and board. A little sticking to the board can be helpful in overcoming the dough's resistance to stretch, so don't over-use flour, and consider using a dough scraper to 'unstick' dough from the board. You may also need to let the partially rolled dough sit for a few minutes to 'relax' and allow for further rolling. At this point, hand-stretching may also help, followed by additional rolling. Place the rolled-out dough onto a pizza peel liberally covered with wholemeal flour.

6. Cover half the dough round with the cheese-spinach mixture, leaving a 2.5cm/1in-border at the edge. Using a pastry brush, wet the border with water. Fold the bare side of the dough over the cheese mixture and seal the border by pinching closed with your fingers. Cut three slits in the top crust, all the way through the dough, using a serrated knife. No resting time is needed.

7. Slide the calzone directly onto the hot stone. Pour 250ml/8 fl oz of hot tap water into the grill tray, and quickly close the oven door. Bake for about 25 minutes, or until golden brown.

8. Allow to cool for 10 minutes before serving to allow the cheese to set a bit.

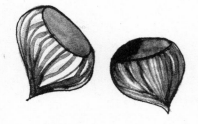

Philadelphia Stromboli with Sausage

Both of us lived briefly in Philadelphia and fondly remember this local speciality. It's really just a folded pizza made with tomatoes, sausage and mozzarella. It was brought to the table still puffed from the oven and glistening with olive oil. Unlike calzone (page 158) or red pepper *fougasse* (page 170), this is a flatbread that is meant to puff exuberantly, like pitta bread, so don't slit the top crust prior to baking.

Makes 1 medium-size stromboli to serve 2 to 4.

Use any of these refrigerated pre-mixed doughs: Boule (page 44), European Peasant (page 66), Olive Oil (page 150), Light Wholemeal (page 94) or Italian Semolina (page 100).

• 450g/1lb (grapefruit-size portion) of any pre-mixed dough listed above
• 50g/2oz canned chopped tomatoes, well drained
• 1 sweet or hot Italian sausage, grilled and cut into 3mm/⅛in-thick slices
• 10 basil leaves, torn or cut into thin ribbons
• 225g/8oz fresh mozzarella cheese, preferably buffalo milk, sliced
• Extra virgin olive oil, for brushing on top
• Wholemeal flour or parchment paper for pizza peel, see page 29

1. Twenty minutes before baking, preheat the oven to 230°C/gas mark 8, with a baking stone set near the middle of the oven (consider a longer preheat if you're finding your results to be denser than you like, see page 34). Place an empty grill tray on any other shelf that won't interfere with the rising stromboli.

2. Dust the surface of the refrigerated dough with flour and cut off a 450g/1lb (grapefruit-size) piece. Dust the piece with more flour and quickly shape it into a ball by stretching the surface of the dough around to the bottom on all four sides, rotating the ball a quarter turn as you go.

3. Flatten the dough with your hands and a rolling pin on a wooden board to produce a 3mm/⅛in-thick round, dusting lightly with flour, as needed, to keep the dough from sticking to the rolling pin and board. A little sticking to the board can be helpful in overcoming the dough's resistance to stretch, so don't over-use flour, and consider using a dough scraper to 'unstick' dough from the board. You may also need to let the partially rolled dough sit for a few minutes to 'relax' and allow for further rolling. At this point, hand-stretching may also help, followed by additional rolling. Place the rolled-out dough onto a pizza peel, liberally covered with wholemeal flour.

4. Cover half the dough round with the tomato, sausage, basil and then the cheese, leaving a 2.5cm/1in border at the edge.

5. Using a pastry brush, wet the border with water. Fold the bare side of dough over the cheese and seal the border by pinching closed with your fingers. Do not slit or slash the dough; stromboli is meant to puff. Brush the top crust with olive oil. No resting or rising time is needed

6. Slide the stromboli directly onto the hot stone. Pour 250ml/8 fl oz of hot tap water into the grill tray, and quickly close the oven door. Bake for about 25 minutes, or until golden brown.

7. Allow to cool for 10 minutes before serving.

Prosciutto and Olive Oil Flatbread

'My friend Ralph's mother comes from Naples, and she remembers a bread from her childhood that was studded with pieces of pork. The lardo from the pork melted into the bread and created a fantastic rich crumb. The bread was called pane di lardo.

'Since your local supermarket isn't likely to carry Italian-style pork, we decided to try a more universally loved Italian meat. Prosciutto is a somewhat expensive, aged, Italian ham. Spanish serrano ham is close to prosciutto in style, and can also be used. The meat lends an incredible combination of sweet and savoury that's nicely complemented by the rosemary. Serve this with chilled Prosecco, Italian sparkling wine, for a sublime appetiser.' – Jeff

Makes 6 appetiser portions.

- 450g/1lb (grapefruit-size portion) Olive Oil dough (page 150)
- ¼ tsp dried rosemary, crumbled, or ½ tsp fresh
- 50g/2oz sliced prosciutto or *serrano* ham, cut into 2.5cm/1in squares
- Extra virgin olive oil, for brushing on top
- Polenta or parchment paper for pizza peel, see page 29
- Cornflour wash (see box, page 73)

1. Dust the surface of the refrigerated dough with flour and cut off a 450g/1lb (grapefruit-size) piece. Dust the piece with more flour and quickly shape it into a ball by stretching the surface of the dough around to the bottom on all four sides, rotating the ball a quarter turn as you go. Using your hands and a rolling pin, flatten it to a thickness of about 1cm/½in.

2. Layer the meat onto the dough round and sprinkle it with the crumbled rosemary. Roll up the dough and shape into a ball. Flatten the ball to a thickness of approximately 2.5cm/1in, and allow to rest and rise on a polenta-covered pizza peel for 40 minutes, though consider a longer rest time if you're finding your results to be denser than you like, see page 39, (or just 20 minutes if you're using fresh, unrefrigerated dough). Consider a longer rest time if you're finding your results to be denser than you like, see page 39.

3. Thirty minutes before baking time, preheat the oven to 200°C/gas mark 6, with a baking stone placed near the middle of the oven (consider a longer preheat if you're finding your results to be denser than you like, see page 34). Place an empty grill tray on any other shelf that won't interfere with the rising bread.

4. Just before baking, brush with cornflour wash and slash a deep cross, scallop or criss-cross pattern into the top, using a serrated bread knife.

5. Slide the loaf directly onto the hot stone. Pour 250ml/8 fl oz of hot tap water into the grill tray, and quickly close the oven door. Bake for about 25 minutes, or until richly browned and firm.

6. Allow to cool before cutting into wedges and eating.

Pissaladière

When Julia Child revealed that much of the French repertoire could be mastered by casual home chefs in *Mastering the Art of French Cooking* (1961), she included a delightful recipe for *Pissaladière Niçoise,* an onion tart with anchovies and black olives in a rich pastry shell. As served in the south of France, this dish is often based on a rustic flatbread or pizza base rather than a pastry shell, so we adapted Julia's recipe for our approach. The original called for dry black Niçoise-style olives but we've found we like it just as well with black olives done in the wetter, Greek Kalamata style. We like fresh, bulk-sold olives, but use whatever you like. Pre-pitted olives have a bit less flavour but they're a timesaver. This makes a great summertime hors d'oeuvre, served with dry white wine.

Makes 6 appetiser portions.

Use any of these refrigerated pre-mixed doughs: Boule (page 44), European Peasant (page 66), Olive Oil (page 150), Light Wholemeal (page 94) or Italian Semolina (page 100).

- 450g/1lb (grapefruit-size portion) of any pre-mixed dough listed above
- 3 medium onions, finely chopped
- 4 tbsp olive oil
- 4 parsley sprigs, chopped
- ¼ tsp dried thyme, or ½ tsp fresh
- ½ bay leaf
- 2 large garlic cloves, chopped
- ½ tsp salt (decrease according to taste, see page 25)
- Freshly ground pepper to taste
- 8 anchovy fillets, from a can or jar, chopped
- 16 pitted Niçoise or Kalamata olives, halved

1. Thirty minutes before baking time, preheat the oven with a baking stone at 250°C/gas mark 9 (consider a longer preheat if you're finding your results to be denser than you like, see page 34). Shelf placement is not critical, and you don't need a grill tray since you won't be using steam.

2. Sauté the onions in olive oil with the herbs, garlic, salt and pepper over medium-low heat until barely browned, about 30 minutes. Don't over-brown, or they will burn while baking.

3. Dust the surface of the refrigerated dough with flour and cut off a 450g/1lb (grapefruit-size) piece. Dust the piece with more flour and quickly shape it into a ball by stretching the surface of the dough around to the bottom on all four sides, rotating the ball a quarter turn as you go.

4. Flatten the dough with your hands and a rolling pin on a clean surface to produce a 3mm/⅛in-thick round, dusting lightly with flour, as needed, to keep the dough from sticking to the rolling pin and board. A little sticking to the board can be helpful in overcoming the dough's resistance to stretch, so don't over-use flour and consider using a dough scraper to 'unstick' dough from the board. You may also need to let the partially rolled dough sit for a few minutes to 'relax' and allow for further rolling. At this point, hand-stretching may also help, followed by additional rolling. Place the rolled-out dough onto a pizza peel liberally covered with polenta.

5. Remove the bay leaf and spread the onion mixture and its oil over the dough. Scatter the anchovies and olives on top. If you have an extractor fan, turn it on now, because some of the polenta will burn at this temperature (see box, page 151).

6. Slide the pissaladière directly onto the hot stone; it may take a number of back-and-forth shakes to dislodge it. Check for browning in 8 to 10 minutes. At this time you may have to turn the pissaladière around to achieve even cooking. It may need up to 5 more minutes in the oven.

7. Cool slightly, cut into wedges or squares and serve.

Focaccia with Onion and Rosemary

Here's the ultimate Tuscan hors d'oeuvre, with onion and rosemary topping on an olive oil dough. Try it with something simple, like rustic antipasto, or as an accompaniment to soups or pastas.

We bake onion *focaccia* at a slightly lower temperature than usual to avoid burning the onions, and we bake it on a baking sheet rather than a baking stone since the oil absorbs into the stone and creates an annoying problem with kitchen smoke that can continue into the next several baking sessions.

The key to success with this recipe is to go light on the onion. If you completely cover the dough surface with onions, the *focaccia* just won't brown and the result, though delicious, will be pale.

Makes 6 appetiser portions.

Use any of these refrigerated pre-mixed doughs: Olive Oil dough is our first choice (page 150), but you can also use Boule (page 44), European Peasant (page 66), Light Wholemeal (page 94), or Italian Semolina (page 100).

- Olive oil for greasing the baking sheet
- 450g/1lb (grapefruit-size portion) of any pre-mixed dough listed above
- ¼ medium white or yellow onion, thinly sliced
- 2 tbsp extra virgin olive oil, plus 1 tsp for drizzling
- ¾ tsp dried rosemary leaves (or 1½ tsp fresh)
- Coarse grain salt and freshly ground pepper for sprinkling on top

1. Twenty minutes before baking, preheat the oven to 220°C/gas mark 7, with an empty grill tray on any shelf that won't interfere with the *focaccia* (consider a longer preheat if you're finding your results to be denser than you like, see page 34). The baking stone is not essential when using a baking sheet; if you omit the stone the preheat can be as short as 5 minutes.

2. Grease a baking sheet with a bit of olive oil or line with parchment paper or a silicone mat. Set aside. Dust the surface of the refrigerated dough with flour and cut off a 450g/1lb (grapefruit-size) piece. Dust the piece with more flour and quickly shape it into a ball by stretching the surface of the dough around to the bottom on all four sides, rotating the ball a quarter turn as you go.

3. Flatten it into a 1–2cm/½–¾in-thick round, using your hands and/or a rolling pin and a minimal amount of flour. Place the round on the prepared baking sheet.

4. Sauté the onion slices in the 2 tablespoons of olive oil until softened but not browned; if you brown them they'll burn in the oven. Strew the onion sparingly over the surface of the dough, leaving a 2.5cm/1in border at the edge. Allow the majority of the dough surface to show through the onions as bare dough. (You may have leftover onion at the end.) If you can't see most of the dough surface, you're using too much onion and your *focaccia* won't brown attractively.

5. Sprinkle with rosemary, coarse grain salt and freshly ground pepper. Finish with a light drizzle of the remaining olive oil over the surface, about 1 tsp, but not so much that it starts dripping off the sides. (As with the onion, you won't cover the whole surface with oil.)

6. Allow the *focaccia* to rest and rise for 20 minutes.

7. After the *focaccia* has rested, place the baking sheet on a rack near the centre of the oven. Pour 250ml/8 fl oz of hot tap water into the grill tray and quickly close the oven door. Bake for about 25 minutes, or until the crust is medium brown. Be careful not to burn the onions. The baking time will vary according to the *focaccia's* thickness. *Focaccia* will not develop a crackling crust, because of the olive oil.

8. Cut into wedges and serve warm.

Olive Fougasse

Provençal *fougasse* and Italian *focaccia* share a linguistic and culinary background. It's said that both may have Ancient Greek or Etruscan roots. *Fougasse* distinguishes itself with artful cutouts that resemble a leaf or ladder; this delivers a crusty result, with lots more surface exposed to the oven heat. As with *focaccia*, it's best to bake it on a baking sheet to prevent oil from being absorbed into your baking stone. The halved olives infuse the dough with their essence.

Makes 6 appetiser portions.

Use any of these refrigerated pre-mixed doughs: Olive Oil (page 150), Boule (page 44), European Peasant (page 66), Light Wholemeal (page 94), or Italian Semolina (page 100).

- 450g/1lb (grapefruit-size portion) of any pre-mixed dough listed above
- 50g /2oz high-quality black olives, preferably Niçoise or Kalamata, pitted and halved or quartered if large
- Olive oil for greasing the baking sheet and brushing the *fougasse*

1. Thirty minutes before baking time, preheat the oven to 200°C/gas mark 6 (consider a longer preheat if you're finding your results to be denser than you like, see page 34). Place an empty grill tray on any other shelf that won't interfere with rising bread. Grease a baking sheet with a bit of olive oil. Set aside. The baking stone is not essential for breads made on a baking sheet; if you omit it the preheat can be as short as 5 minutes.

2. Dust the surface of the refrigerated dough with flour and cut off a 450g/1lb (grapefruit-size) piece. Dust the piece with more flour and quickly shape it into a ball by stretching the surface of the dough around to the bottom on all four sides, rotating the ball a quarter turn as you go.

3. Flatten the mass of dough to a thickness of about 1cm/½in on a wooden board dusted with flour and sprinkle it with olives. Roll up the dough, Swiss roll style, then shape it into a ball. Form a flat round approximately 1cm/½in thick. Because you will need to be able to cut slits into the dough that do not immediately close up and re-adhere to each other, this dough needs to be drier than most; so use flour accordingly. Place the round on a wooden board liberally dusted with flour.

4. Cut angled slits into the circle of dough. You may need to add more flour to be able to cut the slits and keep them spread adequately during baking so they don't close up. Gently pull the holes to open them.

5. Gently lift the slitted dough round onto the prepared greased baking sheet and brush additional olive oil onto the dough. Allow it to rest for 20 minutes.

6. Place the baking sheet with the *fougasse* near the middle of the oven. Pour 250ml/8 fl oz of hot tap water into the grill tray and quickly close the oven door. Check progress after about 20 minutes and continue baking, as needed, until golden brown, which may be 5 minutes longer. *Fougasse* will not develop a crackling crust because of the olive oil.

7. Serve warm.

Fougasse Stuffed with Roasted Red Pepper

This is a very festive folded flatbread with a roasted red pepper filling. It uses some of the same techniques used in making the olive *fougasse*, but the dough is folded after slitting, on one side only, to reveal the roasted red pepper layered inside. The rich and smoky red pepper perfumes the whole loaf. It's a fantastic and impressive hors d'oeuvre, sliced or just broken into pieces.

Makes 6 appetiser portions.

Use any of these refrigerated pre-mixed doughs: Olive Oil (page 150), Boule (page 44), European Peasant (page 66), Light Wholemeal (page 94), or Italian Semolina (page 100).

- 450g/1lb (grapefruit-size portion) of any pre-mixed dough listed above
- 1 medium red pepper (or substitute equivalent amount of jarred roasted red pepper, drained and patted dry)
- Coarse grain salt, for sprinkling
- ¼ tsp dried thyme
- Olive oil, preferably extra virgin, for brushing over the loaf
- Wholemeal flour or parchment paper for pizza peel, see page 29

1. Cut the pepper into quarters and then flatten the pieces, making additional cuts if needed to flatten. Grill the pepper under the grill or on a gas or charcoal barbecue, with the skin side closer to the heat source. Check often and remove when the skin is blackened, 8 to 10 minutes or more, depending on the heat source.

2. Drop the roasted pieces into an empty bowl and cover. The skin will loosen from the steam over the next 10 minutes.

3. Gently peel the pepper by hand and discard the blackened skin; some dark bits will adhere to the pepper flesh, which is fine.

4. Thirty minutes before baking time, preheat the oven to 230°C/gas mark 8, with a baking stone placed near the middle of the oven (consider a longer preheat if you're finding your results to be denser than you like, see page 34). Place an empty grill tray on any other shelf that won't interfere with the rising bread.

5. Dust the surface of the refrigerated dough with flour and cut off a 450g/1lb (grapefruit-size) piece. Dust the piece with more flour and quickly shape it into a ball by stretching the surface of the dough around to the bottom on all four sides, rotating the ball a quarter turn as you go.

6. Using a rolling pin, form a large flat round approximately 3mm/⅛in thick. Add a little more flour than usual when cloaking, shaping and rolling the dough, because you will need to be able to cut slits into the dough that do not close and immediately re-adhere to one another. Place the round on a wholemeal-covered pizza peel.

7. Cut angled slits into the circle of dough on only one half of the round. You may need to add more flour to decrease stickiness so the slits stay open during handling. Gently spread the holes open with your fingers.

8. Cut the roasted pepper into strips, and place in a single layer on the unslit side of the *fougasse*, leaving a 2.5cm/1in border at the edge. Sprinkle with coarse grain salt and thyme. Dampen the dough edge, fold the slitted side over to cover the peppers, and pinch to seal. The peppers should peek brightly through the slitted windows. Brush the loaf with olive oil.

9. Slide the *fougasse* directly onto the hot stone. Pour 250ml/8 fl oz of hot tap water into the grill tray, and quickly close the oven door. Bake for about 25 minutes, or until golden brown.

10. Allow to cool, then slice or break into pieces and serve.

Sweet Provençal Flatbread
with Anise Seeds

Provençal bakers are justly famous for their savoury flatbreads such as Pissaladière (page 164), but their lesser-known, gently sweetened breads are just as delicious. The anise, which has a distinctive liquorice flavour, is a perfect complement to the orange zest.

Makes about four 450g/1lb loaves or 8 small triangular loaves.
The recipe is easily doubled or halved.

- 550ml/18 fl oz water
- 120ml/4 fl oz orange juice
- 3 tbsp olive oil
- 1½ tbsp granulated yeast (decrease according to taste, see page 23)
- 1½ tbsp coarse grain salt (decrease according to taste, see page 25)
- 1 tbsp whole anise seeds for dough, plus more for topping
- 40g/1½oz sugar
- Zest from half an orange
- 900g/2lb plain flour
- Polenta or parchment paper for pizza peel, see page 29
- Cornflour wash (see box, page 73)

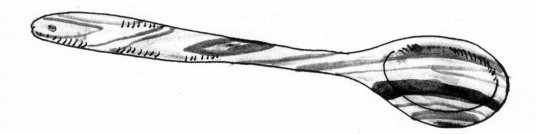

1. Mixing and storing the dough: mix together the yeast, salt, anise seeds, sugar and orange zest with all the liquid ingredients in a 5 litre/8¾ pint bowl, or a lidded (not airtight) food container.

2. Mix in the flour without kneading, using a spoon, a 3.5 litre/6 pint-capacity food processor (with dough attachment), or a heavy-duty stand mixer (with dough hook). If you're not using a machine, you may need to use wet hands to incorporate the last bit of flour.

3. Cover (not airtight), and allow to rest at room temperature until the dough rises and collapses (or flattens on top), approximately 2 hours.

4. The dough can be used immediately after the initial rise, though it is easier to handle when cold. Refrigerate in a lidded (not airtight) container and use over the next 14 days.

5. On baking day, dust the surface of the refrigerated dough with flour and cut off a 450g/1lb (grapefruit-size) piece. Dust the piece with more flour and quickly shape it into a ball by stretching the surface of the dough around to the bottom on all four sides, rotating the ball a quarter turn as you go.

6. Flatten the ball with your hands and then, using a rolling pin and minimal dusting flour, roll out in a round with a uniform thickness of 1cm/½in. Cut the round into several triangles for an authentic Provençal look, or just form into a single round flatbread.

7. Thirty minutes before baking time, preheat the oven to 230°C/gas mark 8, with a baking stone placed on the middle rack (consider a longer preheat if you're finding your results to be denser than you like, see page 34). Place an empty grill tray on any other shelf that won't interfere with the rising bread.

8. Allow the bread to rest and rise on a polenta-covered pizza peel for 20 minutes. Just before baking, paint the surface with cornflour wash and sprinkle with additional anise seeds. If you have shaped a single large loaf, slash it with a serrated knife.

9. Slide the loaf/loaves directly onto the hot stone. Pour 250ml/8 fl oz of hot tap water into the grill tray, and quickly close the oven door. Bake for 15 to 20 minutes, or until richly browned and firm.

10. Allow to cool before eating.

Pine Nut-Studded Polenta Flatbread

Here's another recipe that plays with some classic Italian flavours: pine nuts, polenta and olive oil. Coarse-ground Northern Italian-style polenta creates a marvellous texture and crunch, the pine nuts add richness and flavour, and olive oil pulls it all together. You can make this with Broa dough (page 102), but the flavour will be more subtle and the texture less crunchy. The bread is a natural for dipping into hearty soups, or for dips and hors d'oeuvres.

Makes four 450g/1lb loaves. The recipe is easily doubled or halved.

- 750ml/1¼ pints water
- 1½ tbsp granulated yeast (decrease according to taste, see page 23)
- 1½ tbsp coarse grain salt (decrease according to taste, see page 25)
- 75g/3oz pine nuts
- 75g/3oz polenta
- 800g/1¾lb plain flour
- Olive oil for brushing the top

1. Mixing and storing the dough: mix the yeast, salt and pine nuts with the water in a 5 litre/8¾ pint bowl, or a lidded (not airtight) food container.

2. Mix in the remaining dry ingredients without kneading, using a spoon, a 3.5 litre/6 pint-capacity food processor (with dough attachment), or a heavy-duty stand mixer (with dough hook). If you're not using a machine, you may need to use wet hands to incorporate the last bit of flour.

3. Cover (not airtight), and allow to rest at room temperature until the dough rises and collapses (or flattens on top), approximately 2 hours.

4. The dough can be used immediately after the initial rise, though it is easier to handle when cold. Refrigerate in a lidded (not airtight) container and use over the next 8 days.

5. On baking day, dust the surface of the refrigerated dough with flour and cut off a 450g/1lb (grapefruit-size) piece. Dust the piece with more flour and quickly shape it into a ball by stretching the surface of the dough around to the bottom on all four sides, rotating the ball a quarter turn as you go.

6. Flatten the ball and shape a 2.5cm/1in-thick free-form loaf. Place on a polenta or polenta-covered pizza peel. Press the pine nuts back into the dough if they're peeking out (they will burn if directly exposed to oven heat). Brush with olive oil. Allow to rest and rise for 40 minutes (consider a longer rest time if you're finding your results to be denser than you like, see page 39).

7. Thirty minutes before baking time, preheat the oven to 200°C/gas mark 6, with a baking stone placed on the middle rack (consider a longer preheat if you're finding your results to be denser than you like, see page 34). Place an empty grill tray on any other shelf that won't interfere with the rising bread.

8. Slide the loaf directly onto the hot stone. Pour 250ml/8 fl oz of hot tap water into the grill tray, and quickly close the oven door. Bake for about 20 minutes, or until richly browned and firm.

9. Allow to cool before eating.

Za'atar Flatbread

Za'atar spice has a lemony earthiness that is a bracing departure from everyday Western flavours. The distinctive taste comes from the ground sumac berries mixed with dried thyme and sesame seeds. You can blend your own or buy it at a Middle Eastern shop. To make your own, mix together 1 part ground sumac berries, 2 parts dried thyme, and 1 part sesame seeds.

'I first had za'atar bread in Minneapolis at an Iraqi grocery. The flavour of the spice mixture was so memorable that years later I returned to find the stuff and bake my own. The shopkeeper smiled at my pronunciation, but I was now the proud owner of a very reasonably priced three-year supply of za'atar.' – Jeff

Don't worry if you end up with a large supply of *za'atar* spice blend – we have more recipes in the book where you can use it up. Jim's Spicy Kebabs (page 180) and *Fattoush*, the beautiful bread salad (page 181) are two Mediterranean dishes that get their exciting flavour from *za'atar*.

Makes 1 flatbread.

Use any of these refrigerated pre-mixed doughs: Boule (page 44), European Peasant (page 66), Light Wholemeal (page 94), Olive Oil (page 72), or Italian Semolina (page 100).

- 450g/1lb (grapefruit-size portion) of any pre-mixed dough listed above
- 3 tbsp high-quality extra virgin olive oil, plus more for greasing the tin
- 1 tbsp *za'atar* spice mix (see introduction above)
- Coarse grain salt to taste

1. Grease a baking sheet with a bit of olive oil and set aside. Dust the surface of the refrigerated dough with flour and cut off a 450g/1lb (grapefruit-size) piece. Dust the piece with more flour and quickly shape it into a ball by stretching the surface of the dough around to the bottom on all four sides, rotating the ball a quarter turn as you go.

2. Flatten the ball into a round, approximately 1–2cm/½–¾in thick. Place the round on an olive oil-greased baking sheet.

3. Sprinkle the *za'atar* spice mix over the dough round. Using your fingertips, poke holes into the surface of the dough at approximately 2.5cm/1in intervals. The holes may partially 're-fill' with dough as soon as fingers are removed.

4. Drizzle the oil over the surface of the dough, taking care to fill indentations that remain from your finger-poking (do this even if you've started with olive oil dough). Some of the oil will run off the surface and find its way under the bread. Finish with a sprinkling of coarse grain salt, which strikingly accentuates the sourness of the *za'atar*. Use salt sparingly if your *za'atar* spice blend already contains salt.

5. Thirty minutes before baking time, preheat the oven to 230°C/gas mark 8 (consider a longer preheat if you're finding your results to be denser than you like, see page 34). Place an empty grill tray on any other shelf that won't interfere with the flatbread. The baking stone is not essential with the baking sheet; if you omit it, the preheat may be as short as 5 minutes.

6. After the *za'atar* bread has rested 20 minutes, place the baking sheet on a rack near the centre of the oven. Pour 250ml/8 fl oz of hot tap water into the grill tray and quickly close the oven door.

7. Check the bread at 15 minutes, and continue baking until medium brown. The baking time will vary according to the thickness of the *za'atar* bread. *Za'atar* bread does not develop a crackling crust because of its oil content, but the final colour should be a medium brown.

8. Cut into wedges and serve warm.

Pitta

Pitta bread is the puffy, flour-dusted flatbread of the Middle East. It is a simple and elemental bread, and for reasons we can't explain at all, it's just about our most fragrant one. Aside from being delicious, this bread is among the fastest in the book to make. It's quite easy to produce beautiful puffed loaves. The secret to the puffing is to roll the dough thinly and use a very hot oven. Because pitta isn't slashed, internal steam is trapped inside. As soon as the top and bottom crusts set, steam in the interior pushes them apart. It can't miss! And this is a bread that when still warm from the oven is best.

'My friend Jim has become something of an expert on great pitta, because his job takes him to the Middle East all the time. When he invited my family to his cabin in northern Minnesota, he asked me to prepare pitta to accompany a kebab dish he was making – a special recipe he'd fallen for overseas. It was a delicious incongruity: hot and spicy food from the desert, served with pitta, in northern Minnesota in January. We cross-country skied and hiked all day on the lake, not around it. As the northern sun started to wane, Jim drove out on the ice to summon me back to the kitchen to start on the breads. We made the za'atar flatbread as an appetiser, and puffed pitta for Jim's kebabs. The flavours and smells of the Mediterranean transported us to a different, warmer place.' – Jeff

Makes 1 large family-style pitta, or 4 individual pittas.

Use any of these refrigerated pre-mixed doughs: Boule (page 44), European Peasant (page 66), Light Wholemeal (page 94), or Italian Semolina (page 100).

- 450g/1lb (grapefruit-size portion) of any pre-mixed dough listed above
- Flour for dusting

1. Twenty minutes before baking, preheat the oven to 250°C/gas mark 9 with a baking stone (consider a longer preheat if you're finding your results to be denser than you like, see page 34). You won't be using a grill tray and shelf placement of the stone is not crucial.

2. Just before baking, dust the surface of the refrigerated dough with flour and cut off a 450g/1lb (grapefruit-size) piece. Dust the piece with more flour and quickly shape it into a ball by stretching the surface of the dough around to the bottom on all four sides, rotating the ball a quarter turn as you go. Place the dough on a flour-dusted pizza peel.

3. Using your hands and a rolling pin, roll the dough out into a round with a uniform thickness of 3mm/⅛in throughout. This is crucial, because if it's too thick, it may not puff. You'll need to sprinkle the peel lightly with white flour as you work, occasionally flipping the bread to prevent sticking to the rolling pin or to the board. Use a dough scraper to remove the round of dough from the peel if it sticks. Do not slash the pitta or it will not puff. No rest/rise time is needed. (If you are making individual pittas, form, roll and shape the rest.)

4. If you have an extractor fan, turn it on now because stray flour may smoke at this temperature. Slide the loaf directly onto the hot stone (it may take a number of back-and-forth shakes to dislodge the pitta). Bake for about 5 to 7 minutes, until lightly browned and puffed. You may need to transfer the pitta to a higher shelf (without the stone) to achieve browning.

5. For the most authentic, soft-crusted result, wrap in clean cotton dish towels and set on a cooling rack when baking is complete. The pittas will deflate slightly as they cool. The space between crusts will still be there, but may have to be nudged apart with a fork.

6. Serve the pitta with Jim's Spicy Kebabs (page 180). Or, once the pittas are cool, store in plastic bags. Unlike hard-crusted breads, pitta is not harmed by airtight storage.

Jim's Spicy Kebabs

Jim recreated the flavours he fondly remembered from the Middle East. The meat combination yields succulent morsels, and they're a perfect fit for oven-fresh pitta.

Serves 4 to 6.

- 675g/1½lb minced meat (half lamb and half veal, or all lamb)
- 2 tsp cayenne pepper
- 2 tsp ground cumin seeds
- 2 tsp ground coriander seeds
- 2 tsp ground pepper
- Salt to taste
- Ground sumac or mixed *za'atar* spice (see page 176), to taste, optional
- 1 medium red onion, thinly sliced
- Finely chopped fresh parsley
- 4 to 6 individual pittas (see page 178)

1. Mix all the ingredients except the sumac, onions, parsley and pittas. Cover and let the mixture rest in the fridge for 1 hour.

2. Prepare a charcoal barbecue or preheat a gas barbecue on medium-low for 15 minutes. Form the meat into elongated patties and barbecue, without overcooking and turning often, until the kebabs are springy to the touch, about 20 minutes.

3. Fill the pitta halves with the patties and sprinkle lightly with sumac. Top with the sliced onions and garnish with the chopped parsley.

Fattoush

This Lebanese bread salad is as beautiful to look at as it is to eat, with all its rich colours and exotic Middle Eastern flavours. *Fattoush* is related to other Mediterranean bread salads like *Tuscan Panzanella* (page 68), which is always based on European bread. This Lebanese speciality has some differences from the Tuscan variety. The flavour is defined by lemon juice, mint, parsley and, if you have it, sumac or *za'atar* (see Za'atar Flatbread, page 176). The salad calls for Middle Eastern pitta bread (page 178), which is used fresh and toasted, rather than stale as in *Panzanella* – stale pittas turn really solid when you toast them!

Makes 4 servings

The Salad

- 3 medium tomatoes, cubed
- 1 medium cucumber, chopped
- 1 spring onion, sliced into rings
- 2 large romaine lettuce leaves, torn into bite-size pieces
- 15g/½oz finely chopped parsley
- 3 tbsp chopped fresh mint, or 1 tbsp dried
- 2 pittas (page 178), about 15–20cm/ 6–8in across, toasted crisp and cut into bite-size chunks

The Dressing

- 5 tbsp extra virgin olive oil
- Juice of ½ lemon
- 1 garlic clove, finely chopped
- 1 tsp salt (decrease according to taste, see page 25)
- Freshly ground pepper to taste
- 1 tsp ground sumac or *za'atar* (see page 176)

1. Prepare all the ingredients for the salad and place in a large salad bowl.

2. Whisk all the ingredients for the dressing until well combined.

3. Pour the dressing over the salad and allow to stand for at least 10 minutes, or until the bread has softened.

Lavash

Armenian *lavash* is believed to be among the world's oldest breads, dating back as many as ten thousand years. This simple flatbread makes a great vehicle to mop up sauces, or serve with soups and dips.

The small amount of dough goes a long way because it's rolled so thin. There are thicker versions from other parts of Central Asia as well as superthin cracker versions. We pull our *lavash* from the oven when only lightly browned and still chewy. Like so many other things, this is a matter of taste, so if you're looking for a cracker bread, bake it until deep brown and crispy. Experiment with several doughs. This is a very versatile recipe.

The flavours that hit you in our *lavash* are sesame seeds and the bread's light caramelisation. The combination outweighs the usual 'wheatiness' of most breads, making this a very unique, yet subtle flavour experience.

Makes several *lavash*.

Use any of these refrigerated pre-mixed doughs: Boule (page 44), European Peasant (page 66), Light Wholemeal (page 94), Italian Semolina (page 100) or Olive Oil (page 150).

• 225g/8oz (orange-size portion) of any pre-mixed dough listed above
• Sesame seeds for top crust
• Cornflour wash (see box, page 73)

1. Twenty minutes before baking, preheat the oven to 230°C/gas mark 8, with a baking stone (consider a longer preheat if you're finding your results to be denser than you like, see page 34). Place an empty grill tray on any other shelf that won't interfere with the bread.

2. Meanwhile, dust the surface of the refrigerated dough with flour and cut off a 225g/8oz (orange-size) piece. Dust the piece with more flour and quickly shape it into a ball by stretching the surface of the dough around to the bottom on all four sides, rotating the ball a quarter turn as you go.

3. Place the dough on a pizza peel and shape it into a flat round, using your hands and a rolling pin. Continue rolling out the bread on the peel until you reach a uniform thickness of 1.5–3mm/¹⁄₁₆–⅛in throughout. You'll be able to make several lavash from your 225g/8oz piece of dough.

4. Brush the top surface with cornflour wash and sprinkle with sesame seeds. Prick the surface all over with a fork to allow steam to escape and prevent puffing. There's no need for resting time.

5. Slide the lavash directly onto the hot stone. Pour 250ml/8 fl oz of hot tap water into the grill tray, and quickly close the oven door. Bake for about 5 minutes, or until lightly browned. Do not overbrown; you're not trying to crisp the bread.

6. Lavash cools quickly; but can be served warm. Once cool, it stores very well in plastic bags. Unlike hard-crusted breads, lavash is not harmed by airtight storage.

Ksra (Moroccan Anise and Barley Flatbread)

This is a very hearty and satisfying country bread that is virtually unknown in the United States. If you can't get rolled barley or barley flour, substitute wholemeal or rye flour; either will blend nicely with the anise. Moroccan flatbreads are thicker than *lavash* and pitta. We make ours about the same thickness as our *focaccia*.

'I first tasted ksra on a bus in 1987. The bus, however, was 1960s vintage, and it bumped painfully over the Atlas Mountains of Morocco. The rest stops didn't include restaurants, the bus was freezing at high altitude, and the ride was much longer than billed, so I was starving. At a rest stop, I bought some ksra from a street vendor. If you're going to live through an adventure like this on bread and water for 16 hours, this is the most delicious way to do it. The heartiness of the barley made it feel like a meal.' – Jeff

Makes four 450g/1lb loaves. The recipe is easily doubled or halved.

- 750ml/1¼ pints lukewarm water
- 1½ tbsp granulated yeast (decrease according to taste, see page 23)
- 1½ tbsp salt (decrease according to taste, see page 25)
- 1 tbsp whole anise seeds
- 105g/3¾oz rolled barley or barley flour
  (wholemeal or rye can be substituted)
- 800g/1¾lb unbleached plain flour
- Polenta or parchment paper for pizza peel, see page 29

1. Mixing and storing the dough: mix the yeast, salt and anise seeds with the water in a 3 litre/5 pint bowl, or a lidded (not airtight) food container.

2. Mix in flours without kneading, using a spoon, a 3.5 litre/6 pint-capacity food processor (with dough attachment), or a heavy-duty stand mixer (with dough hook). If you're not using a machine, you may need to use wet hands to incorporate the last bit of flour.

3. Cover (not airtight), and allow to rest at room temperature until the dough rises and collapses (or flattens on top), approximately 2 hours.

4. The dough can be used immediately after the initial rise, though it is easier to handle when cold. Refrigerate in a lidded (not airtight) container and use over the next 10 days.

5. On baking day, preheat the oven to 230°C/ gas mark 8, with a baking stone placed on the middle rack. Place an empty grill tray on any other shelf that won't interfere with the bread.

6. Dust the surface of the refrigerated dough with flour and cut off a 450g/1lb (grapefruit-size) piece. Dust the piece with more flour and quickly shape it into a ball by stretching the surface of the dough around to the bottom on all four sides, rotating the ball a quarter turn as you go.

7. Flatten the dough into a 2cm/¾in-thick round and allow to rest and rise on a polenta-covered pizza peel for 20 minutes.

8. Slide the loaf directly onto the hot stone. Pour 250ml/8 fl oz of hot tap water into the grill tray, and quickly close the oven door. Bake for about 20 minutes, or until richly browned and firm.

9. Allow to cool, cut into wedges and serve.

Chilled Moroccan-Style Gazpacho

Of course, one cannot really live on *ksra* and water alone, so here's
something to go with our hearty Moroccan bread (see page 184).
We love the light, refreshing coolness of garden-fresh *gazpacho* on
a summer evening, but we wanted a soup that was more like a meal.
We borrowed the chickpeas and spicy *harissa* paste from Moroccan
harira soup and *voilà!* A smooth, tangy chilled soup with a North
African accent.

Makes 4 servings.

- 3 ripe medium tomatoes
- ½ medium cucumber, roughly chopped
- 1 red pepper, roughly chopped
- 2 slices bread
- ½ small onion, roughly chopped
- 2 cloves garlic, roughly chopped
- 2 tbsp red wine vinegar
- 5 tbsp extra virgin olive oil
- ½ tsp ground cumin
- 1 tsp salt (decrease according to taste, see page 25)
- Freshly ground black pepper to taste
- 3 tsp harissa paste
- 15g/½oz chopped coriander
- 1 can chickpeas, well-drained

1. Place all ingredients except chickpeas into the bowl of a food processor and process until desired consistency; we like ours a bit chunky, but purists will insist it should be smooth – your choice.

2. Add chickpeas and allow to stand for 30 minutes in the fridge. Adjust seasonings just before eating.

Suvir Saran's Chilled Yogurt Soup with Cucumber and Mint

'My friend Suvir Saran, chef/owner of the acclaimed New York restaurant Dévi, ingeniously merges very traditional Indian flavours with the most sophisticated modern cuisine. This recipe comes from his sublime book Indian Home Cooking. The cool and soothing yogurt blended with bracing spices is a provocative way to start off a summertime meal, served with fresh, soft naan, glistening with ghee (see page 190).' – Zoë

Makes 4 servings.

- 1½ tsp cumin seeds
- 750g/1lb 10oz plain yogurt
- 1 medium cucumber, roughly chopped
- 1 small fresh hot green chilli, seeded and finely chopped
- ¼ tsp garam masala
- 1 tsp salt, or to taste
- ⅛ tsp freshly ground white pepper
- 3 tbsp roughly chopped fresh mint leaves,
  plus 12 additional whole leaves for garnish

1. Toast the cumin seeds in a dry frying pan
   or saucepan over medium heat for 2 to 3
   minutes, until lightly browned and fragrant.
   Grind to a powder in a spice grinder.

2. Reserving a small amount of cumin powder
   for the garnish, combine all ingredients except
   the whole mint leaves in a food processor
   and process until smooth. Scrape the mixture
   into a serving bowl. Refrigerate for at least
   30 minutes, until chilled.

3. To serve, garnish with whole mint leaves and
   sprinkle with ground cumin, if desired.

Naan

This delicious and buttery Indian flatbread is traditionally made in a huge cylindrical clay tandoori oven, with the wet dough slapped directly onto the oven's hot walls. Our naan is done in a hot, cast-iron frying pan, or a heavyweight non-stick frying pan. Butter or oil will work in lieu of authentic Indian clarified butter (*ghee*), but the taste won't be as authentic.

This recipe also has the distinction of producing the fastest bread in the book, since it's cooked on the hob without an oven preheat (*lavash* and pitta are close seconds). As with many of our flatbreads, there's no need to rest the dough. You can easily make one of these just before dinner, even on busy nights (so long as you have the dough in the fridge). Try it with Suvir Saran's Chilled Yogurt Soup with Cucumber and Mint (page 188).

'Naan has become my family's favourite bread to make while camping in the woods. All we need is a 30cm/12in cast-iron frying pan on our sturdy Coleman stove to have freshly baked bread. We always attract a crowd of curious campers drawn to the aroma wafting amidst the wood smoke.' – Jeff

Makes 1 naan.

Use any of these refrigerated pre-mixed doughs: Boule (page 44), European Peasant (page 66), Light Wholemeal (page 94), Italian Semolina (page 100).

- 115g/4oz (peach-size portion) of any pre-mixed dough listed above
- 1 tbsp *ghee*, or neutral-flavoured oil
- Butter for brushing on loaf if *ghee* is unavailable

1. Dust the surface of the refrigerated dough with flour and cut off a 115g/4oz (peach-size) piece. Dust the piece with more flour and quickly shape it into a ball by stretching the surface of the dough around to the bottom on all four sides, rotating the ball a quarter turn as you go. Using your hands and a rolling pin, and minimal flour, roll out to a uniform thickness of 3mm/⅛in throughout and to a diameter of 20–23cm/8–9in.

2. Heat a heavy 30cm/12in cast-iron frying pan over high heat on the hob. When water droplets flicked into the pan skitter across the surface and evaporate quickly the pan is ready. Add the *ghee* or oil, pouring out excess fat if necessary.

3. Drop the rolled dough round into the frying pan, decrease the heat to medium, and cover the frying pan to trap the steam and heat.

4. Check to see if it is ready, with a spatula, at about 3 minutes, or sooner if you're smelling overly quick browning. Adjust the heat as needed. Flip the naan when the underside is richly browned.

5. Continue cooking another 2 to 6 minutes, or until the naan feels firm, even at the edges, and the second side is browned. If you've rolled a thicker naan, or if you're using dough with whole grains, you'll need more pan time.

6. Remove the naan from the pan, brush with butter if the dough was cooked in oil, and serve.

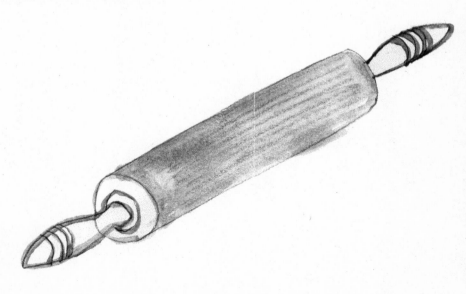

Flatbrød

We developed a quick version of traditional Scandinavian rye crisp bread. It is usually baked unadorned, but in an unorthodox mood we added some Mediterranean zest by topping it with olive oil and coarse grain salt. Unlike our *lavash, flatbrød* is rolled out paperthin, then baked till crisp and browned. Top with smoked fish, herring, capers or other Scandinavian delicacies and serve.

Makes several sheets of crisp *flatbrød.*

- 225g/8oz (orange-size portion) Deli-Style Rye dough (page 80), mixed without caraway seeds
- Olive oil for brushing
- Coarse grain salt for sprinkling

1. Twenty minutes before baking, preheat the oven to 190°C/gas mark 5, with a baking stone (consider a longer preheat if you're finding your results to be denser than you like, see page 34). Place an empty grill tray on any other shelf that won't interfere with the bread.

2. Dust the surface of the refrigerated dough with flour and cut off a 225g/8oz (orange-size) piece. Dust the piece with more flour and quickly shape it into a ball by stretching the surface of the dough around to the bottom on all four sides, rotating the ball a quarter turn as you go.

3. Place the dough on a pizza peel and shape the dough into a flat round, approximately 2.5cm/1in thick. Cut the dough into several small pieces and roll out on the pizza peel until it is paperthin, adding plain flour as needed. You should be able to make several *flatbrød* from your 225g/8oz piece of dough.

4. Brush the breads with olive oil and sprinkle with coarse grain salt. Prick the surface all over with a fork to allow steam to escape and prevent puffing. There's no need for resting time.

5. Slide the *flatbrød* directly onto the hot stone. Pour 250ml/8 fl oz of hot tap water into the grill tray, and quickly close the oven door. Check for puffing at 5 minutes; if you see any large bubbles puffing up, prick them with a sharp fork. Bake the breads for 15 minutes, or until richly browned and crisp. Repeat the process to make the rest of the crisp breads.

6. Allow to cool on a rack and break into serving-size portions.

ENRICHED BREADS
AND PASTRIES

We're particularly pleased to present great sweet enriched breads and pastries made from stored dough. If you keep enriched dough in your freezer, you'll be able to store it for weeks. Then, create great morning pastries, coffee cakes, holiday breads and late-night chocolate fixes on the spur of the moment. Though some of them need a few minutes more preparation than our regular breads, they're all based on dough that will be stored, so the preparation time will be a fraction of what you're used to with traditional pastries, and you'll have wonderful results. Enjoy!

Challah

This is the bread traditionally served in Jewish households at the start of the Sabbath on Friday nights. Some variation of an egg-enriched sweet loaf appears across bread-loving cultures. The French and Italians have Brioche (page 204). The choice of melted butter versus oil definitely changes the flavour and aroma. And butter-enriched doughs are stiffer and easier to plait when cold; oil-based challah dough is a little 'looser' and more prone to spreading sideways while resting, but delicious nonetheless. For an intense and decadent challah, try making it with Brioche dough. The blast of butter and egg creates an incredibly rich bread-eating experience.

We store the egg-enriched dough in the freezer after 5 days of fridge storage.

Makes four 450g/1lb loaves. The recipe is easily doubled or halved.

- 400ml/14 fl oz lukewarm water
- 1½ tbsp granulated yeast (decrease according to taste, see page 23)
- 1½ tbsp coarse grain salt (decrease according to taste, see page 25)
- 4 large eggs, lightly beaten
- 8 tbsp clear honey
- 115g/4oz unsalted butter, melted (or neutral-tasting vegetable oil such as rapeseed), plus more for greasing the baking sheet
- 980g/1lb 3oz unbleached plain flour
- Egg wash (1 egg beaten with 1 tbsp of water)
- Poppy or sesame seeds for the top

1. Mixing and storing the dough: mix the yeast, salt, eggs, honey and melted butter (or oil) with the water in a 5 litre/8¾ pint bowl, or a lidded (not airtight) food container.

2. Mix in the flour without kneading, using a spoon, a 3.5 litre/6 pint-capacity food processor (with dough attachment), or a heavy-duty stand mixer (with dough hook). If you're not using a machine, you may need to use wet hands to incorporate the last bit of flour.

3. Cover (not airtight), and allow to rest at room temperature until the dough rises and collapses (or flattens on top), approximately 2 hours.

4. The dough can be used immediately after the initial rise, though it is easier to handle when cold. Refrigerate in a lidded (not airtight) container and use over the next 5 days. Beyond 5 days, freeze in 450g/1lb portions in an airtight container for up to 4 weeks. Defrost frozen dough overnight in the fridge before using. Then allow the usual rest and rise time.

5. On baking day, butter or grease a baking sheet or line with parchment paper or a silicone mat. Dust the surface of the refrigerated dough with flour and cut off a 450g/1lb (grapefruit-size) piece. Dust the piece with more flour and quickly shape it into a ball by stretching the surface of the dough around to the bottom on all four sides, rotating the ball a quarter turn as you go.

6. Divide the ball into thirds, using a dough scraper or knife. Roll the balls between your hands (or on a board), stretching, to form each into a long, thin rope. If the dough resists shaping, let it rest for 5 minutes and try again. Plait the ropes, starting from the centre and working to one end. Turn the loaf over, rotate it, and plait from the centre out to the remaining end. This produces a loaf with a more uniform thickness than when plaited from end to end.

7. Allow the bread to rest and rise on the prepared baking sheet for 1 hour and 20 minutes (or just 40 minutes if you're using fresh, unrefrigerated dough).

8. Thirty minutes before baking time, preheat the oven to 190°C/gas mark 5 (consider a longer preheat if you're finding your results to be denser than you like, see page 34). If you're not using a stone in the oven, 5 minutes is adequate. Brush the loaf with egg wash and sprinkle with the seeds.

9. Bake near the centre of the oven for about 25 minutes. Smaller or larger loaves will require adjustments in baking time. The challah is done when golden brown, and the plaits near the centre of the loaf offer resistance to pressure. Due to the fat in the dough, challah will not form a hard, crackling crust.

10. Allow to cool before slicing or eating.

Turban-Shaped Challah with Raisins

Turban-Shaped Raisin Challah is served at the Jewish New Year, but similar enriched and fruited egg breads are part of holiday traditions all over the Western world, calling to mind the richer Italian Pannetone, served at Christmas (page 216).

We've assumed in this recipe that you're using stored challah dough and rolling the raisins into it. If you're starting a batch of dough just for raisin challah, add 130g/4½oz of raisins to the yeasted water when mixing.

Makes 1 challah.

Use any of these refrigerated pre-mixed doughs: Challah (page 196) or Brioche (page 204).

- 450g/1lb (grapefruit-size portion) of any pre-mixed dough listed above, defrosted overnight in fridge if frozen
- Butter for greasing baking sheet
- 40g/1½oz raisins
- Egg wash (1 egg beaten with 1 tbsp of water)
- Sesame seeds for the top

1. Defrost the dough overnight in the fridge if frozen. On baking day, grease a baking sheet or line with parchment paper ora silicone mat. Dust the surface of the refrigerated dough with flour and cut off a 450g/1lb (grapefruit-size) piece. Dust the piece with more flour and quickly shape it into a ball by stretching the surface of the dough around to the bottom on all four sides, rotating the ball a quarter turn as you go.

2. Using a rolling pin and minimal dusting flour, roll out the dough to a thickness of 1cm/½ in. Sprinkle with the raisins and roll into a log.

3. Rolling the dough between your hands and stretching it, form a single, long, thin rope, tapering it at one end. If the dough resists shaping, let it rest for 5 minutes and try again.

4. Starting with the thick end of the rope, begin forming a coil on the prepared baking sheet. When you have finished coiling, pinch the thin end under the loaf. Allow to rest and rise for 1 hour and 20 minutes (or just 40 minutes if you're using fresh, unrefrigerated dough).

5. Thirty minutes before baking time, preheat the oven to 190°C/gas mark 5 (consider a longer preheat if you're finding your results to be denser than you like, see page 34). If you're not using a stone in the oven, 5 minutes is adequate.

6. Brush the loaf with egg wash and sprinkle with seeds, and place near the centre of the oven. Bake for about 25 minutes. The challah is done when golden brown and the centre of the loaf offers resistance to pressure. Smaller or larger loaves will require adjustments in baking time. Due to the fat in the dough, challah will not form a hard, crackling crust.

7. Allow to cool before slicing or eating.

John Barrymore Onion Pletzel

'*Pletzel*' or '*pletzl*' is a Yiddish word meaning 'board.' It was a savoury flatbread widely available in Jewish bakeries until about twenty-five years ago. The *pletzel* flavours are a unique blend of onions and poppy seeds baked onto enriched and slightly sweetened dough. It is an Eastern European savoury treat that is unforgettable when served with pot-roasted meats. *Pletzel* is perfect for mopping up that home-style gravy.

'*For reasons that are to this day unclear, my grandfather called this bread "John Barrymore Pletzel". It's too bad I didn't question him about it during his lifetime. I find absolutely no connection between the actor John Barrymore and any bread, let alone pletzel.*

'*This is one of my most vivid taste memories from childhood. Twenty years elapsed between the last time I ate it and the first time I baked it, but the flavour is exactly what I recalled.*' – Jeff

Makes 2 pletzel.

Use any of these refrigerated pre-mixed doughs: Challah (page 196) or Brioche (page 204).

- 450g/1lb (grapefruit-size portion) of any pre-mixed dough listed above, defrosted overnight in fridge if frozen
- 1½ tbsp neutral-tasting oil or 20g/¾oz butter, plus more for greasing the tin
- 1 small onion, thinly sliced
- 2 tsp poppy seeds
- ¼ tsp salt (decrease according to taste, see page 25)

1. On baking day, grease a baking sheet or line with parchment paper or a silicone mat. Set aside. Dust the surface of the refrigerated dough with flour and cut off a 450g/1lb (grapefruit-size) piece. Dust the piece with more flour and quickly shape it into a ball by stretching the surface of the dough around to the bottom on all four sides, rotating the ball a quarter turn as you go.

2. Using a rolling pin or your hands, flatten the dough to a thickness of 1cm/½in and place on the prepared baking sheet. (Alternatively, press the unrolled dough into a well-greased, 23cm/9in square non-stick baking tin.) Allow to rest and rise 20 minutes.

3. Thirty minutes before baking time, preheat the oven to 190°C/gas mark 5 (consider a longer preheat if you're finding your results to be denser than you like, see page 34). If you're not using a stone in the oven, 5 minutes is adequate.

4. Meanwhile, sauté the onion in the oil or butter until very lightly browned; don't overbrown, or they will burn in the oven. Scatter the onions on to the *pletzel* and drizzle oil or butter over them (don't completely cover the surface with onions or the *pletzel* won't brown well). Finish by sprinkling the poppy seeds and salt over the onions.

5. After the *pletzel* has rested, place the baking sheet near the centre of the oven. Bake for 15 to 20 minutes, or until the *pletzel* has browned but the onions are not burned.

6. Allow to cool, then cut into pieces before serving.

201

Sticky Pecan Caramel Rolls

This crowd-pleaser was our first attempt to make dessert from stored bread dough. Stored bread dough? For dessert? We were sceptical, but our first attempt with sweet enriched dough, caramel, toasted nuts and spices was so successful that it reshaped our view of what this cookbook would be. The flavours were actually enhanced by using stored dough. We've even used the Boule dough in this recipe, and it works! The butter and sugar in the filling and on the bottom of the pan seep into the folds and do a pretty good approximation of the egg-enriched version.

Makes 6 to 8 large caramel rolls.

Use any of these refrigerated pre-mixed doughs: Challah (page 196), Brioche (page 204) or Boule (page 44).

• 675g/1½lb (cantaloupe-size portion) of any pre-mixed dough listed above, defrosted overnight in the fridge if frozen

The Caramel Topping
• 75g/3oz unsalted butter, softened
• ½ tsp salt (decrease according to taste, see page 25)
• 115g/4oz brown sugar
• 30 pecan halves

The Filling
• 50g/2oz salted butter, softened
• 50g/2oz sugar
• 1 tsp ground cinnamon
• ¼ tsp freshly grated nutmeg
• 50g/2oz chopped and toasted pecans
• Pinch of ground black pepper

1. On baking day, cream together the butter, salt and brown sugar. Spread evenly over the bottom of a 23cm/9in round cake tin. Scatter the pecans over the butter-sugar mixture and set aside.

2. Dust the surface of the refrigerated dough with flour and cut off a 675g/1½lb (cantaloupe-size) piece. Dust the piece with more flour and quickly shape it into a ball by stretching the surface of the dough around to the bottom on all four sides, rotating the ball a quarter turn as you go.

3. With a rolling pin, roll out the dough to a 3mm/⅛in-thick rectangle. As you roll out the dough, use enough flour to prevent it from sticking to the work surface but not so much as to make the dough dry.

4. Cream together the butter, sugar and spices. Spread evenly over the rolled-out dough and sprinkle with the chopped nuts. Starting with the long side, roll the dough into a log. If the dough is too soft to cut, let it chill for 20 minutes to firm up.

5. With a very sharp serrated knife, cut the log into 8 equal pieces and arrange over the pecans in the pan, with the 'swirled' edge facing upward. Cover loosely with clingfilm and allow to rest and rise 1 hour (or just 40 minutes if you're using fresh, unrefrigerated dough).

6. Thirty minutes before baking time, preheat the oven to 190°C/gas mark 5 (consider a longer preheat if you're finding your results to be denser than you like, see page 34). If you're not using a stone in the oven, 5 minutes is adequate.

7. Bake about 40 minutes, or until golden brown and well set in centre. While still hot, run a knife around the inside of the tin to release the caramel rolls, and invert immediately onto a serving dish. If you let them set too long they will stick to the pan and be difficult to turn out.

Brioche

The doomed Marie Antoinette is often quoted as saying *'qu'ils mangent de la brioche'*, which means 'let them eat brioche', not 'let them eat cake'! Historians believe it was the insensitive remark of an earlier queen, but in any case it was brioche on their minds and not cake.

Brioche is a wonderful bread that everyone should eat. It is enjoyed as a sweet bread with tea or as a breakfast pastry. Brioche is rich with butter (only use butter, never oil), egg and a touch of honey. It is perfect baked in a simple loaf tin or as a *Brioche à Tête* (page 206) and it is also the inspiration for many of our pastry recipes.

Makes four 450g/1lb loaves. The recipe is easily doubled or halved.

- 350ml/12 fl oz lukewarm water
- 1½ tbsp granulated yeast (decrease according to taste, see page 23)
- 1½ tbsp coarse grain salt (decrease according to taste, see page 25)
- 8 eggs, lightly beaten
- 8 tbsp clear honey
- 350g/12oz unsalted butter, melted, plus butter for greasing the tin
- 1.05kg/2lb 5oz unbleached plain flour
- Egg wash (1 egg beaten with 1 tbsp of water)

1. Mix the yeast, salt, eggs, honey and melted butter with the water in a 5 litre/8¾ pint bowl, or a lidded (not airtight) food container.

2. Mix in the flour without kneading, using a spoon, a 3.5 litre/6 pint-capacity food processor (with dough attachment), or a heavy-duty stand mixer (with dough hook). If you're not using a machine, you may need to use wet hands to incorporate the last bit of flour. The dough will be loose but will firm up when refrigerated; don't try to work with it before chilling. (You may notice lumps in the dough but they will disappear in the finished products.)

3. Cover (not airtight), and allow to rest at room temperature until dough rises and collapses (or flattens on top), approximately 2 hours.

4. The dough can be used as soon as it's chilled after the initial rise. Refrigerate in a lidded (not airtight) container and use over the next 5 days. Beyond 5 days, freeze the dough in 450g/1lb portions in an airtight container for up to 4 weeks. When using frozen dough, thaw in the fridge for 24 hours before using, then allow the usual rest and rise times.

5. Defrost the dough overnight in the fridge if frozen. On baking day, grease a 23 x 10 x 7.5cm/9 x 4 x 3in non-stick loaf tin. Dust the surface of the refrigerated dough with flour and cut off a 450g/1lb (grapefruit-size) piece. Dust the piece with more flour and quickly shape it into a ball by stretching the surface of the dough around to the bottom on all four sides, rotating the ball a quarter turn as you go.

6. Elongate into an oval and place in the prepared tin. Allow to rest for 1 hour and 20 minutes.

7. Thirty minutes before baking time, preheat the oven to 190°C/gas mark 5 (consider a longer preheat if you're finding your results to be denser than you like, see page 34). If you're not using a stone in the oven, 5 minutes is adequate.

8. Using a pastry brush, brush the top crust with egg wash.

9. Place the bread near the centre of the oven and bake for 35 to 40 minutes, or until a medium golden brown. Due to the fat in the dough, brioche will not form a hard, crackling crust.

10. Allow to cool before slicing or eating.

Brioche à Tête

Brioche à tête is a very traditional French bread loaf, baked in a beautifully fluted pan and sporting an extra little ball of dough at the top (the *tête*, or head). Your guests will think you slaved over this one. The shape is ubiquitous in Parisian shops but quite rare elsewhere.

Makes 1 loaf.

- 450g/1lb (grapefruit-size portion) Brioche dough (page 204), defrosted overnight in the fridge if frozen
- Butter or oil for greasing the tin
- Egg wash (1 egg beaten with 1 tbsp of water)

1. Grease a brioche tin with a small amount of oil or butter.

2. Dust the surface of the refrigerated dough with flour and cut off a 450g/1lb (grapefruit-size) piece. Break off about an eighth of the dough to form the *tête* (head) and set it aside. Dust the large piece with more flour and quickly shape it into a ball by stretching the surface of the dough around to the bottom on all four sides, rotating the ball a quarter turn as you go.

3. Place the larger ball into the prepared tin, seam side down; the tin should be about half-full. Poke a fairly deep indentation in the top of this ball of dough. This is where you will attach the tête.

4. Quickly shape the small piece into a teardrop shape by rounding one end and tapering the other. Place the teardrop, pointed side down, into the indentation of the dough in the pan and pinch the two together gently but firmly to ensure the *tête* stays attached during baking.

5. Allow to rest at room temperature for 1 hour and 20 minutes.

6. Thirty minutes before baking time, preheat the oven to 190°C/gas mark 5 (consider a longer preheat if you're finding your results to be denser than you like, see page 34). If you're not using a stone in the oven, 5 minutes is adequate.

7. Brush the loaf with egg wash and place it in the centre of the oven. Bake for about 40 minutes, or until golden brown. The amount of dough and baking time will vary depending on the pan size.

8. Remove from brioche mould and cool on a rack, so the crust won't get soggy.

Almond Brioche

We adore this flavoured brioche with its combination of almond cream and orange zest-infused sugar. The traditional method involves baking brioche, slicing it, topping the slices with almond cream and re-baking it. But that's just too much work for our five-minutes-a-day cookbook. We wanted the flavours without the extra work, so we rolled the filling into the dough and baked it just once. It was fantastic!

Makes 1 loaf.

- 675g/1½lb (cantaloupe-size portion) Brioche dough (page 204), defrosted overnight in the fridge if frozen
- 50g/2oz unsalted butter at room temperature, plus more for greasing the tin
- 115g/4oz marzipan
- 35g/1¼oz unbleached plain flour
- 1 egg
- ¼ tsp orange-flower water (optional)
- ¼ tsp almond extract
- 50g/2oz sugar, plus more for dusting the greased tin
- Zest from half an orange
- 50g/2oz flaked almonds

1. Making the almond cream: cream together the butter, marzipan, flour, egg, orange-flower water and almond extract in a food processor until smooth and well combined. Set aside.

2. Assembling the brioche: dust the surface of the refrigerated dough with flour and cut off a 675g/1½lb (cantaloupe-size) piece. Dust the piece with more flour and quickly shape it into a ball by stretching the surface of the dough around to the bottom on all four sides, rotating the ball a quarter turn as you go.

3. With a rolling pin, roll out the ball into a 5mm/¼in-thick rectangle. As you roll out the dough, use enough flour to prevent it from sticking to the work surface but not so much as to make the dough dry.

4. Spread the almond cream evenly over the rectangle, leaving a 2.5cm/1in border all around. Roll up the dough, Swiss roll style, starting at the long end, and being sure to seal the bare edges. The dough will be very soft, so chill the log for about 15 minutes in the freezer before cutting it in Step 6.

5. Generously grease a 20cm/8in round cake tin with butter. Sprinkle the greased pan with a dusting of granulated sugar.

6. Cut the refrigerated dough into 8 equal pieces. Place them evenly in the prepared cake tin so that the swirled cut edge is facing upwards. Allow the dough to rest for 1 hour.

7. Thirty minutes before baking time, preheat the oven to 190°C/gas mark 5 (consider a longer preheat if you're finding your results to be denser than you like, see page 34). If you're not using a stone in the oven, 5 minutes is adequate.

8. Just before baking, mix together sugar, orange zest and almonds and sprinkle over the brioche. Bake without steam until golden brown and well set in the centre, about 40 minutes.

9. Run a knife around the inside of the tin to release the brioche while it is still hot and invert it onto a serving dish. If you let it set too long it will stick to the pan and be difficult to turn out. Eat warm.

Brioche Filled with Chocolate Ganache

This is the closest you'll ever get to the aroma of a Paris pâtisserie in your own kitchen. Using the best chocolate available makes a difference. As the bread bakes, the chocolate ganache will reveal itself and create a wonderfully rustic-looking loaf.

Makes 1 loaf.

- 450g/1lb (grapefruit-size portion) Brioche dough (page 204), defrosted overnight in the fridge if frozen
- 115g/4oz plain chocolate (Valrhona or equivalent; page 26), finely chopped
- 25g/1oz unsalted butter, plus more for greasing the tin
- 4 tsp cocoa powder
- 1 tbsp rum
- 5 tbsp golden syrup
- 1 egg white, lightly beaten with 1 tbsp water
- Granulated sugar for sprinkling on top

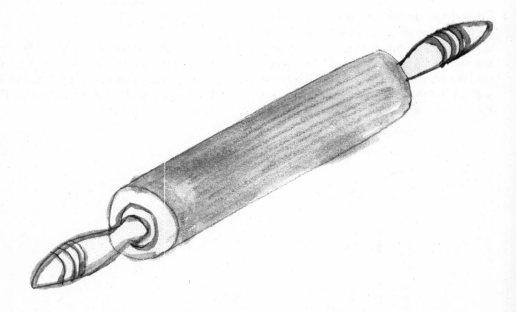

1. Making the ganache: melt the chocolate over a double boiler or in the microwave on low, until smooth. Remove from heat, add the butter, and stir until incorporated.

2. Stir the cocoa powder into the rum, add the golden syrup, and mix until smooth. Add to the chocolate.

3. Assembling the brioche: Lightly butter a 23 x 10 x 7.5cm/9 x 4 x 3in non-stick loaf tin. Dust the surface of the refrigerated dough with flour and cut off a 450g/1lb (grapefruit-size) piece. Dust the piece with more flour and quickly shape it into a ball by stretching the surface of the dough around to the bottom on all four sides, rotating the ball a quarter turn as you go. Using a rolling pin, roll out the ball into a 5mm/¼in thick rectangle, dusting with flour as needed.

4. Spread two-thirds of the ganache evenly over the rectangle, leaving a 2.5cm/1in border all around. Starting at the short end, roll up the dough, being careful to seal the bare edges.

5. Gently tuck the loose ends underneath, elongate into an oval and drop into the prepared tin.

6. Allow to rest 1 hour and 40 minutes.

7. Thirty minutes before baking time, preheat the oven to 190°C/gas mark 5 (consider a longer preheat if you're finding your results to be denser than you like, see page 34). If you're not using a stone in the oven, 5 minutes is adequate. Using a pastry brush, paint the top crust with egg white. Sprinkle lightly with granulated sugar.

8. Bake the brioche for about 45 minutes, or until the top is golden brown and the sugar caramelises. Due to the butter in the dough, the brioche will not form a hard, crackling crust.

9. Remove from the pan and cool slightly; then drizzle the remaining ganache over the top crust. Cool completely and slice.

Beignets

Beignet is French for fritter, or as we Americans like to call them, doughnuts. They're made from rich, yeasted dough, fried in oil and then covered generously in icing sugar. What's not to love? Here's a re-creation using our simple recipe for this sweet confection, made famous by Café Du Monde in New Orleans.

'My husband and I went to New Orleans for a weekend to eat and listen to jazz. Our first stop in town was Café Du Monde. After two orders of fluffy hot beignets and plenty of café au lait, we were covered in icing sugar and ready to find some jazz. We managed to return to Café Du Monde at least once every day during our stay. Thank goodness it was largely spared from Hurricane Katrina, so we will be back.' – Zoë

Makes 5 or 6 beignets.

Use any of these refrigerated pre-mixed doughs: Challah (page 196) or Brioche (page 204).

- 450g/1lb (grapefruit-size portion) of either pre-mixed dough shown above, defrosted overnight in the fridge if frozen
- Vegetable oil for deep frying
- Icing sugar

Special Equipment
- Deep saucepan for frying, or an electric fryer
- Slotted spoon
- Paper towels
- Sugar thermometer

1. Dust the surface of the refrigerated dough with flour and cut off a 450g/1lb (grapefruit-size) piece. Dust the piece with more flour and quickly shape it into a ball by stretching the surface of the dough around to the bottom on all four sides, rotating the ball a quarter turn as you go.

2. Roll the dough into a 1cm/½in-thick rectangle on a lightly floured surface. Using a pizza cutter or knife, cut the dough into 5cm/2in squares. Allow the dough to rest for 15 to 20 minutes.

3. Meanwhile, fill the saucepan (or electric fryer) with at least 7.5cm/3in of oil. Bring the oil to 185°C as determined by the sugar thermometer.

4. Carefully drop the beignets in the hot oil 2 or 3 at a time so they have plenty of room to float to the surface. Do not overcrowd, or they will not rise nicely.

5. After 2 minutes, gently flip the beignets over with a slotted spoon and fry for another minute or until golden brown on both sides.

6. Using the slotted spoon, remove the beignets from the oil and place them on paper towels to drain.

7. Repeat with the remaining dough until all the beignets are fried.

8. Dust generously with icing sugar and eat with a fresh cup of café au lait.

Chocolate or Jam-Filled Beignets

As if the traditional beignets weren't decadent enough, we felt compelled to fill them with chocolate or jam. They are quite simple to make and everyone who eats them becomes a little bit happier.

Makes 5 or 6 beignets.

Use any of these refrigerated pre-mixed doughs: Challah (page 196) or Brioche (page 204).

- 450g/1lb (grapefruit-size portion) of either pre-mixed dough shown above, defrosted overnight in the fridge if frozen
- Vegetable oil for deep frying
- 115g/4oz semi-sweet chocolate, cut into 15g/½oz pieces, or 4 tbsp of your favourite jam
- Icing sugar

Special Equipment
- Deep saucepan for frying, or an electric fryer
- Slotted spoon
- Paper towels
- Sugar thermometer

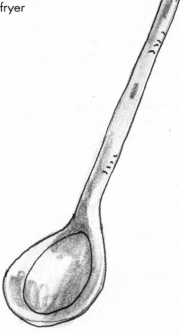

1. Dust the surface of the refrigerated dough with flour and cut off a 450g/1lb (grapefruit-size) piece. Dust the piece with more flour and quickly shape it into a ball by stretching the surface of the dough around to the bottom on all four sides, rotating the ball a quarter turn as you go.

2. Roll the dough into a 5mm/¼in-thick rectangle on a lightly floured surface. Using a pizza cutter or knife, cut the dough into 5cm/2in squares, then place 15g/½oz piece of chocolate or a teaspoon of jam in the centre of each square. Gather the edges of the dough around the filling, pinching at the centre to form a seal. If you are not able to seal the edges very well, use a small amount of water to help stick them together.

3. Allow the beignets to rest for 15 to 20 minutes while the oil heats up to 185°C as determined by the sugar thermometer.

4. Carefully drop the beignets in the hot oil, 2 or 3 at a time so they have plenty of room to rise to the surface. Do not overcrowd or they will not rise nicely.

5. After 2 minutes, gently flip the beignets over with a slotted spoon and fry for another minute or until golden brown on both sides.

6. Using the slotted spoon, remove the beignets from the oil and drain on paper towels. Repeat with the remaining dough until all the beignets are fried.

7. Dust generously with icing sugar and eat with a fresh cup of café au lait.

Panettone

Panettone is the classic Christmas bread sold all over Italy during the holidays. It finds its origins in Milan around the fifteenth century, and has been the subject of much lore. The most often told story of how this bejewelled bread came to be goes something like this: A young nobleman falls in love with a baker's daughter named Toni. The nobleman disguises himself as a pastry chef's apprentice and creates the tall fruit-studded bread to present to Toni, calling it 'Pan de Toni'. The bread is a success in the bakery and the father blesses the marriage.

The story is rich and fanciful, just like the bread, made with dried fruit and the essence of lemons and vanilla. There are traditional *panettone* moulds that are very high sided and come either straight or fluted. You can use a brioche mould, but the bread won't have the classic high sides.

Makes three 675g/1½lb loaves. The recipe is easily doubled or halved.

- 350ml/12 fl oz lukewarm water
- 1½ tbsp granulated yeast (decrease according to taste, see page 23)
- 1½ tbsp coarse grain salt (decrease according to taste, see page 25)
- 8 tbsp clear honey
- 8 eggs, lightly beaten
- 225g/8oz unsalted butter, melted, plus more for greasing the tin
- 1 tsp lemon extract
- 2 tsp vanilla extract
- 2 tsp lemon zest
- 1.05kg/2lb 5oz unbleached plain flour
- 350g/12oz mixed dried fruit, chopped (sultanas, dried pineapple, dried apricots, dried cherries and mixed peel, just to name a few that we've tried and loved in this bread)
- Egg wash (1 egg beaten with 1 tbsp of water)

1. Mixing and storing the dough: mix the yeast, salt, honey, eggs, melted butter, extracts and zest with the water in a 5 litre/8¾ pint bowl, or a lidded (not airtight) food container.

2. Mix in the flour and dried fruit without kneading, using a spoon, a 3.5 litre/6 pint-capacity food processor (with dough attachment), or a heavy-duty stand mixer (with dough hook). If you're not using a machine, you may need to use wet hands to incorporate the last bit of flour. The dough will be loose, but will firm up when refrigerated (don't try to use it without chilling).

3. Cover (not airtight), and allow to rest at room temperature until the dough rises and collapses (or flattens on top), approximately 2 hours.

4. The dough can be used as soon as it's chilled after the initial rise, or frozen for later use. Refrigerate in a lidded (not airtight) container and use over the next 5 days. Beyond that, freeze the dough in 450g/1lb pound portions in an airtight container up to 4 weeks. When using frozen dough, thaw in the fridge for 24 hours before using, then allow the usual rest and rise time.

5. On baking day, grease a *panettone* or brioche tin with a small amount of butter.

6. Dust the surface of the refrigerated dough with flour and cut off a 675g/1½lb (cantaloupe-size) piece. Dust the piece with more flour and quickly shape it into a ball by stretching the surface of the dough around to the bottom on all four sides, rotating the ball a quarter turn as you go. Place the ball into the pan, seam side down.

7. Loosely cover the dough with oiled clingfilm and allow to rest at room temperature for 1 hour and 40 minutes.

8. Thirty minutes before baking time, preheat the oven to 190°C/gas mark 5 (consider a longer preheat if you're finding your results to be denser than you like, see page 34). The baking stone is not essential for loaf-tin breads; if you omit it, the preheat may be as short as 5 minutes.

9. Remove the clingfilm and brush the *panettone* with egg wash. Bake in the centre of the oven without steam for 50 to 55 minutes, or until golden brown and hollow sounding when tapped. The amount of dough and baking times will vary depending on the pan size.

10. Allow to cool before slicing or eating.

Soft American-Style White Bread

American-style sliced white bread doesn't get a lot of respect from serious bread lovers. Most of our experience with it is based on plastic-wrapped products, often chemically preserved on the shelf for long periods of time. But it doesn't have to be this way. With this recipe you can produce something much nicer.

While many people will be happy with the Crusty White Sandwich Loaf (page 62), some kids will want a bread with a softer crust. What they're hankering after is the fat – that's what keeps commercial crusts so soft. We chose to use plain old butter in ours, and a little sugar for tenderness. Try it with our grilled Croque Monsieur French ham and cheese sandwich (page 220).

Makes three 675g/1½lb loaves. The recipe is easily doubled or halved.

- 750ml/1¼ pints lukewarm water
- 1½ tbsp granulated yeast (decrease according to taste, see page 23)
- 1½ tbsp coarse grain salt (decrease according to taste, see page 25)
- 2 tbsp sugar
- 115g/4oz unsalted butter, melted, plus additional for brushing the top crust
- 980g/1lb 3oz unbleached plain flour
- Neutral-tasting oil or softened butter for greasing baking tin

1. Mixing and storing the dough: mix the yeast, salt, sugar and melted butter with the water in a 5 litre/8¾ pint bowl, or a lidded (not airtight) food container.

2. Mix in the flour without kneading, using a spoon, a 3.5 litre/6 pint-capacity food processor (with dough attachment), or a heavy-duty stand mixer (with dough hook). If you're not using a machine, you may need to use wet hands to incorporate the last bit of flour.

3. Cover (not airtight), and allow to rest at room temperature until the dough rises and collapses (or flattens on top), approximately 2 hours.

4. The dough can be used immediately after the initial rise with only a 40-minute rest in the tin, though it is easier to handle when cold. Refrigerate the remaining dough in a lidded (not airtight) container and use over the next 7 days.

5. On baking day, lightly grease a 23 x 10 x 7.5cm/9 x 4 x 3in non-stick loaf tin. Dust the surface of the refrigerated dough with flour and cut off a 675g/1½lb (cantaloupe-size) piece. Dust the piece with more flour and quickly shape it into a ball by stretching the surface of the dough around to the bottom on all four sides, rotating the ball a quarter turn as you go. Elongate the ball into an oval.

6. Drop the dough into the prepared tin. You want to fill the pan slightly more than half full.

7. Allow the dough to rest for 1 hour and 40 minutes (or just 40 minutes if you're using fresh, unrefrigerated dough). Dust the loaf with flour and slash the top, using the tip of a sharp knife. Brush the top surface with melted butter.

8. Thirty minutes before baking time, preheat the oven to 180°C/gas mark 4 (consider a longer preheat if you're finding your results to be denser than you like, see page 34). If you're not using a stone in the oven, 5 minutes is adequate. A baking stone is not essential when using a loaf tin.

9. Bake the bread near the centre of the oven for about 45 minutes, or until golden brown.

10. Allow to cool completely before slicing, or it will be nearly impossible to achieve reasonable sandwich slices.

Croque Monsieur

This classic Parisian street food is a hearty and simple sandwich. Start with freshly baked sandwich bread, slather it with Dijon mayonnaise, add some Gruyère cheese and ham, and then fry it in butter. Serve it with a glass of light red wine and a salad for a little bit of heaven.

Makes 1 sandwich.

- 1½ tbsp mayonnaise
- 2 tsp whole-grain Dijon mustard
- 2 slices sandwich loaf bread (page 218)
- 10g/¼oz butter, plus more if needed
- 40g/1½oz Gruyère cheese
- 50g/2oz thinly sliced ham

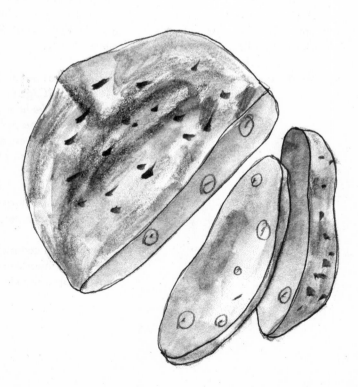

1. Blend together the mayonnaise and mustard; set aside.

2. Butter one side of each slice of bread, and spread the other side with the mustard-mayonnaise mixture. Place one slice of bread, butterside down, in a frying pan.

3. Cover with half the cheese, then the ham. Finish with the other half of the cheese.

4. Place the frying pan over medium-low heat and fry slowly for approximately 4 minutes per side, or until browned and crisp. Add additional butter to the pan if needed.

Buttermilk Bread

Many traditional American and British breads use buttermilk, which tenderises the bread, creating a lovely soft crust and crumb, and a terrific flavour. It makes an ideal sandwich loaf, and it's heavenly in Judy's Board of Directors' Cinnamon-Raisin Bread (page 224). You can also use this dough in place of any of the Boule dough recipes in The Master Recipe Chapter, lowering the baking temperature to 190°C/gas mark 5.

Makes three 675g/1½lb loaves. The recipe is easily doubled or halved.

- 475ml/16 fl oz lukewarm water
- 250ml/8 fl oz buttermilk
- 1½ tbsp granulated yeast (decrease according to taste, see page 23)
- 1½ tbsp coarse grain salt (decrease according to taste, see page 25)
- 1½ tbsp sugar
- 900g/2lb unbleached plain flour
- Butter or neutral-tasting oil for greasing the tin

1. Mixing and storing the dough: mix the yeast, salt and sugar with the water and buttermilk in a 5 litre/8¾ pint bowl, or a lidded (not airtight) food container.

2. Mix in the flour without kneading, using a spoon, a 3.5 litre/6 pint-capacity food processor (with dough attachment), or a heavy-duty stand mixer (with dough hook). If you're not using a machine, you may need to use wet hands to incorporate the last bit of flour.

3. Cover (not airtight), and allow to rest at room temperature until the dough rises and collapses (or flattens on top), approximately 2 hours.

4. The dough can be used immediately after the initial rise, though it is easier to handle when cold. Refrigerate in a lidded (not airtight) container and use over the next 7 days.

5. On baking day, lightly grease a 23 x 10 x 7.5cm/9 x 4 x 3in non-stick loaf tin. Dust the surface of the refrigerated dough with flour and cut off a 675g/1½lb (cantaloupe-size) piece. Dust the piece with more flour and quickly shape it into a ball by stretching the surface of the dough around to the bottom on all four sides, rotating the ball a quarter turn as you go. Elongate the ball into an oval.

6. Drop the dough into the prepared tin. You want to fill the tin slightly more than half full.

7. Allow the dough to rest for 1 hour and 40 minutes (or just 40 minutes if you're using fresh, unrefrigerated dough). Dust the loaf with flour and slash the top, using the tip of a sharp knife. Brush the top surface with melted butter.

8. Thirty minutes before baking time, preheat the oven to 190°C/gas mark 5 (consider a longer preheat if you're finding your results to be denser than you like, see page 34). If you're not using a stone in the oven, 5 minutes is adequate. A baking stone is not essential when using a loaf tin.

9. Bake the bread near the centre of the oven for about 45 minutes, or until golden brown.

10. Remove from the tin. Allow to cool completely before slicing, or it will be nearly impossible to achieve reasonable sandwich slices.

Judy's Board of Directors' Cinnamon-Raisin Bread

'My friend Judy is the C.E.O. of a successful company. She has a passion for bread that she brings into the boardroom. At one tense meeting with her Board of Directors, she used the simple magic of shaping loaves to win over sceptical board members. She slammed the dough onto the conference table.

"Growing a company," Judy told them, "is like baking bread. Sometimes you have to be patient, and wait for the dough to rise. You can't rush it. Things need to develop spontaneously, on their own."

'She shaped a loaf, pushing and prodding. The loaf was formed – cinnamon-raisin bread! And the Board gave its blessing to the company's next stage. She's continued to serve this bread, with butter and jam, at all kinds of business meetings, tense or otherwise.' – Jeff

We've adapted Judy's recipe for our quick method. As always with our dough, don't bother kneading (unless you're trying to intimidate your Board).

Makes three 675g/1½lb loaves. The recipe is easily doubled or halved.

- 675g/1½lb (cantaloupe-size portion) Buttermilk Bread dough (page 222)
- Butter or neutral-tasting oil for greasing the tin
- 1½ tsp ground cinnamon
- 130g/4½oz raisins
- Egg wash (1 egg beaten with 1 tbsp water)

1. Lightly grease a 23 x 10 x 7.5cm/9 x 4 x 3in non-stick loaf tin. Set aside. Dust the surface of the refrigerated dough with flour and cut off a 675g/1½lb (cantaloupe-size) piece. Dust the piece with more flour and quickly shape it into a ball by stretching the surface of the dough around to the bottom on all four sides, rotating the ball a quarter turn as you go.

2. With a rolling pin, roll out the dough to an 20 x 40cm/8 x 16in rectangle about 5mm/¼in thick, dusting the board and rolling pin with flour as needed. You may need to use a metal dough scraper to loosen rolled dough from the board as you are working with it.

3. Using a pastry brush, cover the surface of the dough lightly with egg wash. Mix together the sugar and cinnamon and sprinkle the mixture evenly over the dough. Evenly distribute the raisins.

4. Starting from the short side, roll it up Swiss roll style. Pinch the edges and ends together, tucking the ends under.

5. Place the loaf seam side down in the prepared tin. Allow to rest 1 hour and 40 minutes (or just 40 minutes if you're using fresh, unrefrigerated dough).

6. Thirty minutes before baking time, preheat the oven to 190°C/gas mark 5 (consider a longer preheat if you're finding your results to be denser than you like, see page 34). If you're not using a stone in the oven, 5 minutes is adequate. The stone is not essential when using a loaf tin.

7. Bake for 35 to 40 minutes, or until golden brown.

8. Remove from pan and allow to cool before slicing.

Chocolate Bread

Chocolate bread is found in artisan bakeries all over the country. Its origin is unknown, but we'd like to thank the chocoholic who found yet another way to satisfy our chocolate cravings. The honey is subtle, allowing chocolate's bittersweet notes to come through. It's not chocolate cake; it's better, and much less ordinary. The texture says bread, but chocolate cake lovers won't be disappointed.

Makes two 675g/1½lb loaves. The recipe is easily doubled or halved.

- 115g/4oz premium plain chocolate, preferably Valrhona or equivalent
- 115g/4oz unsalted butter
- 400ml/16 fl oz lukewarm water
- 1½ tbsp granulated yeast (decrease according to taste, see page 23)
- 1½ tbsp coarse grain salt (decrease according to taste, see page 25)
- 4 large eggs, lightly beaten
- 10 tbsp clear honey
- 770g/1lb 11oz unbleached plain flour
- 115g/4oz cocoa powder, preferably Valrhona or equivalent
- 140g/5oz finely chopped plain chocolate, preferably Valrhona or equivalent
- Butter or neutral-tasting oil for greasing the baking sheet

1. Making the ganache: melt the 115g/4oz of chocolate and the butter in a double-boiler or microwave until chocolate is melted. Blend together and set aside.

2. Mixing and storing the dough: mix the yeast, salt, eggs and honey with the water in a 5 litre/8¾ pint bowl, or a lidded (not airtight) food container.

3. Mix in the flour, cocoa powder, ganache and the 140g/5oz of chocolate without kneading, using a spoon, a 3.5 litre/6 pint-capacity food processor (with dough attachment), or a heavy-duty stand mixer (with dough hook). If you're not using a machine, you may need to use wet hands to incorporate the last bit of flour.

4. Cover (not airtight), and allow to rest at room temperature until the dough rises and collapses (or flattens on top), approximately 2 hours.

5. The dough can be used immediately after the initial rise, though it is easier to handle when cold. Refrigerate in a lidded (not airtight) container and use over the next 5 days. Beyond 5 days, freeze the dough in 450g/1lb portions in an airtight container for up to 4 weeks. When using frozen dough, thaw in the fridge for 24 hours before using, then allow the usual rest and rise time.

6. On baking day, line a baking sheet with parchment paper or a silicone mat. Dust the surface of the refrigerated dough with flour and cut off a 675g/1½lb (canteloupe-size) piece. Dust the piece with more flour and quickly shape it into a ball by stretching the surface of the dough around to the bottom on all four sides, rotating the ball a quarter turn as you go.

7. Allow the ball to rest and rise on the prepared baking sheet for 1 hour and 40 minutes (or just 40 minutes if you're using fresh, unrefrigerated dough). Paint with egg wash.

8. Thirty minutes before baking time, preheat the oven to 190°C/gas mark 5 (consider a longer preheat if you're finding your results to be denser than you like, see page 34). If you're not using a stone in the oven, 5 minutes is adequate. The stone is not essential when using a baking sheet.

9. Place the bread in the centre of the oven and bake for about 35 minutes. Smaller or larger loaves will require adjustments in baking time.

10. Remove from pan. Allow to cool before slicing or eating.

Swiss Muesli Breakfast Bread

This dough will be wet and sticky when you are mixing it, but will be easier to handle once you chill it. And it bakes up with a glorious moist texture. The final result makes for a hearty breakfast bread, which is slightly sweet and wonderful with preserves.

Makes one 675g/1½lb loaf.

- 675g/1½lb (cantaloupe-size portion) Challah (page 196) or Brioche dough (page 204) defrosted overnight in the fridge if frozen
- 75g/3oz Swiss muesli
- 120ml/4 fl oz milk
- Egg wash (1 egg beaten with 1 tbsp of water)
- Wholemeal flour or parchment paper for pizza peel, see page 29

1. On baking day, mix together the Swiss muesli and the milk and allow to stand for 10 minutes.

2. Dust the surface of the refrigerated dough with flour and cut off a 675g/1½lb (cantaloupe-size) piece. Place it into a bowl. Using your hands, blend the muesli into the dough; this will be reminiscent of making mud pies!

3. Dust the piece with more flour and quickly shape it into a ball by stretching the surface of the dough around to the bottom on all four sides, rotating the ball a quarter turn as you go.

4. Allow the ball to rest for 1 hour and 40 minutes on a flour-covered pizza peel (or just 40 minutes if you're using fresh, unrefrigerated dough).

5. Using a pastry brush, brush the top crust with egg wash.

6. Thirty minutes before baking time, preheat the oven to 190°C/gas mark 5, with a baking stone placed on a middle rack (consider a longer preheat if you're finding your results to be denser than you like, see page 34).

7. Bake the loaf directly on the stone without steam for about 30 minutes until golden brown. Due to the fat in the dough, the bread will not form a hard, crackling crust.

8. Allow to cool before slicing or eating.

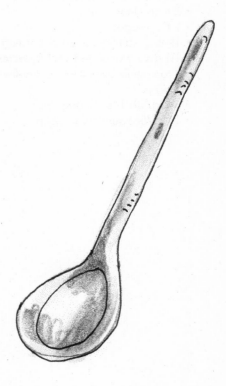

Sunflower Seed Breakfast Loaf

'Thomas Gumpel, my bread instructor and friend from the Culinary Institute of America, inspired this recipe. The first time I made the bread in his class was under some duress. I'd been a bit impertinent during a lecture and he decided to make an example of my kitchen misdemeanour. He had me mix the sunflower bread in an old-fashioned 'bread bucket' (circa 1900) in the dining hall as public humiliation. The process took the better part of the class period, and my pride, albeit strong, took some abuse. But the bread was sublime. As harrowing as my first experience with this bread was, I've always loved to make it, but now it takes only a fraction of the time to prepare.' – Zoë

Makes three 675g/1½lb loaves. The recipe is easily doubled or halved.

- 475ml/16 fl oz lukewarm milk
- 8 tbsp clear honey
- 2 tbsp sugar
- 1½tbsp salt (decrease according to taste, see page 25)
- 1½ tbsp granulated yeast (decrease according to taste, see page 23)
- 4 tbsp sunflower oil (or neutral-flavoured oil), plus more for greasing the tin
- 3 eggs
- 840g/1lb 14oz strong flour
- 140g/5oz sunflower seeds

1. Mixing and storing the dough: mix the honey, sugar, salt, yeast, sunflower oil and eggs with the lukewarm milk in a 5 litre/8¾ pint bowl, or a lidded (not airtight) food container.

2. Mix in the flour and sunflower seeds without kneading, using a spoon, a 3.5 litre/ 6 pint-capacity food processor (with dough attachment), or a heavy-duty stand mixer (with dough hook). If you're not using a machine, you may need to use wet hands to incorporate the last bit of flour. Add the sunflower seeds to the dough.

3. Cover (not airtight), and allow to rest at room temperature until the dough rises and collapses (or flattens on top), approximately 2 hours.

4. The dough can be used immediately after the initial rise, though it is easier to handle when cold. Refrigerate in a lidded (not airtight) container and use over the next 5 days, or store the dough for up to 4 weeks in the freezer in loaf-sized portions.

5. On baking day, lightly grease a 23 x 10 x 7.5cm/9 x 4 x 3in non-stick loaf tin. Cut off and form a 675g/1½lb cylinder and place in the tin. Allow to rest and rise for 1 hour and 40 minutes (or just 40 minutes if you're using fresh, unrefrigerated dough).

6. Thirty minutes before baking time, preheat the oven to 190°C/gas mark 5 (consider a longer preheat if you're finding your results to be denser than you like, see page 34). The baking stone is not essential for loaf-tin breads; if you omit it, the preheat may be as short as 5 minutes.

7. Place the bread in the centre of the oven and bake for 35 to 40 minutes, without steam, or until golden brown.

8. Remove from tin and allow to cool before slicing or eating.

Chocolate Prune Bread

This bread is a great combination of flavours; it is rich and powerfully chocolatey (especially if you use chocolate dough as the base) without being too sweet.

We think prunes are delicious as well as being nutritious, and they have a marvellous concentrated flavour that says, well, prunes. This bread pairs well with a glass of Armagnac (or a glass of milk!)

Makes one 675g/1½lb loaf.

Use any of these refrigerated pre-mixed doughs: Challah dough (page 196), Brioche dough (page 204), or Chocolate Bread dough (page 226)

- 675g/1½lb (cantaloupe-size portion) of any pre-mixed dough listed above
- Softened butter for greasing the tin
- 175g/6oz chopped high-quality plain chocolate (50g/2oz if using Chocolate Bread dough), preferably Valrhona or equivalent
- 175g/6oz chopped prunes
- Egg wash (1 egg beaten with 1 tbsp of water)
- 4 tbsp sugar for sprinkling over the top of the bread and preparing the tin

1. On baking day, generously grease a 23 x 10 x 7.5cm/9 x 4 x 3in non-stick loaf tin with butter, sprinkle sugar evenly over the butter, and shake the pan to distribute.

2. Dust the surface of the refrigerated dough with flour and cut off a 675g/1½lb (cantaloupe-size) piece. Dust the piece with more flour and quickly shape it into a ball by stretching the surface of the dough around to the bottom on all four sides, rotating the ball a quarter turn as you go. Using a rolling pin, roll out the dough into a 1cm/½in-thick rectangle. As you roll out the dough, use enough flour to prevent it from sticking to the work surface but not so much as to make the dough dry.

3. Sprinkle the chocolate and chopped prunes over the dough and roll the dough up to encase them. Fold the dough over itself several times, turning and pressing it down with the heel of your hand after each turn. This will work the chocolate and prunes into the dough; some may poke through.

4. With very wet hands, form the dough into a loaf shape and place it in the prepared tin. Cover loosely with clingfilm and allow to rest and rise for 1 hour and 40 minutes (or just 40 minutes if you're using fresh, unrefrigerated dough).

5. Thirty minutes before baking time, preheat the oven to 190°C/gas mark 5 (consider a longer preheat if you're finding your results to be denser than you like, see page 34). The baking stone is not essential for loaf-tin breads; if you omit it, the preheat may be as short as 5 minutes. Just before putting the bread in the oven brush the top with egg wash and sprinkle with sugar.

6. Bake the loaf in the centre of the oven, without steam, for 40 to 50 minutes, or until firm. Smaller or larger loaves will require adjustments in baking time.

7. Remove from tin. Allow to cool before slicing or eating.

Chocolate-Raisin Babka

In our babka, based on a Ukrainian recipe, we call for 16 egg yolks, which make it extremely rich and velvety. In the traditional method, the milk and flour are cooked together, and the egg yolks are added one by one – sometimes up to 30 of them! We've simplified the recipe without losing any of the old-fashioned charm. You can freeze the left-over egg whites and use them later to make meringue.

Makes four 450g/1lb loaves. The recipe is easily doubled or halved.

- 750ml/1¼ pints lukewarm milk
- 16 egg yolks
- 1½ tbsp granulated yeast (decrease according to taste, see page 23)
- 90g/3½oz sugar
- 2 tsp salt (decrease according to taste, see page 25)
- 175g/6oz unsalted butter, melted, plus more for greasing the tin
- 1.07kg/2lb 5½oz plain flour
- 130g/4½oz raisins
- 130g/4½oz plain chocolate, finely chopped or grated
- 3 tbsp rum for soaking the baked loaf

1. Mixing and storing the dough: mix the egg yolks, yeast, sugar, salt and melted butter with the milk in a 5 litre/8¾ pint bowl, or a lidded (not airtight) food container.

2. Mix in the flour without kneading, using a spoon, a 3.5 litre/6 pint-capacity food processor (with dough attachment), or a heavy-duty stand mixer (with dough hook). The mixture will be quite loose because of all the yolks.

3. Cover (not airtight), and allow to rest at room temperature until the dough rises and collapses (or flattens on top), approximately 2 hours. Brush rum onto loaf when slightly cooled.

4. Due to all the egg yolks, you must chill the dough before using it. Refrigerate in a lidded (not airtight) container and use over the next 5 days. Beyond five days, freeze the dough in 450g/1lb portions in an airtight container for up to four weeks. When using frozen dough, thaw in fridge for 24 hours before use, then allow the usual rest and rise times.

5. On baking day, grease a 23 x 10 x 7.5cm/ 9 x 4 x 3in non-stick loaf tin. Dust the surface of the refrigerated dough with flour and cut off a 450g/1lb (grapefruit-size) piece. Dust the piece with more flour and quickly shape it into a ball by stretching the surface of the dough around to the bottom on all four sides, rotating the ball a quarter turn as you go.

6. Using a rolling pin, roll the dough into a 5mm/¼in-thick rectangle. Sprinkle the raisins and chocolate evenly over the dough. Roll the dough into a log, starting at the short end. Fold the dough so the two ends meet and form it into a ball.

7. Fill the tin with dough so it is approximately two-thirds full. Allow to rest and rise 1 hour and 40 minutes (or just 40 minutes if you're using fresh, unrefrigerated dough).

8. Thirty minutes before baking time, preheat the oven to 190°C/gas mark 5 The baking stone is not essential for loaf-tin breads; if you omit it, the preheat can be as short as 5 minutes.

9. Place the tin near the centre of the oven (not directly on the stone if you're using one). Bake for about 35 minutes, or until golden brown and firm.

10. Allow to cool before slicing or eating. Brush with rum.

Apple and Pear Coffee Cake

'Every year our family goes to the orchards to pick apples. Here in Minnesota we are blessed with the finest apples I've ever experienced. I like to bake with a combination; some sweet and some tart, some that keep their shape and some that will break down and get saucy. No matter what apple you pick, this recipe will be a favourite. I like to include the pear for the variety of flavour, adding almost a perfumey quality.' – Zoë

Makes 1 coffee cake.

The Streusel Topping
- 115g/4oz oats
- 140g/5oz plain flour
- 225g/8oz brown sugar
- 115g/4oz chopped nuts, optional
- 115g/4oz butter, melted
- Pinch of ground cinnamon

The Cake
- 675g/1½lb (cantaloupe-size portion) Brioche dough (page 204)
- Butter for greasing the tin
- 2 small apples, 1 tart and 1 sweet, thinly sliced
- 1 pear, thinly sliced
- 3 tbsp brown sugar
- Zest of half an orange
- 175g/6oz streusel topping (above)

1. Prepare the topping: combine all streusel ingredients in a bowl and mix until the butter is roughly incorporated. Don't overmix – you want a crumbly texture. Set aside.

2. Assembling the cake: grease a 20cm/8in round cake tin with butter and dust with flour. Set aside.

3. Toss the apples, pear, brown sugar and zest together in a small bowl and set aside.

4. Dust the surface of the chill dough with flour and cut off a cantaloupe-size piece. Dust with more flour and quickly shape it into a rough ball by stretching the surface of the dough around to the bottom on all four sides, rotating the ball a quarter turn as you go.

5. Roll out the dough into a 3mm/⅛in-thick rectangle, approximately 30 x 40cm/12 x 16 in. As you roll out the dough, add flour as needed to prevent sticking.

6. Cut the dough into two 20cm/8in rounds, by tracing the bottom of the cake tin. Save any scraps for Cinnamon Twists and Turns (page 244).

7. Place one of the dough rounds in the bottom of the prepared cake tin. Top with half the apple mixture and then sprinkle half the streusel topping over it. Repeat with next layer of dough, apple mixture and streusel.

8. Rest the cake for 1 hour and 20 minutes.

9. Thirty minutes before baking time, preheat the oven to 190°C/gas mark 5 (consider a longer preheat if you're finding your results to be denser than you like, see page 34). The baking stone is not essential for bread baked in a tin; if you omit it, the preheat can be as short as 5 minutes.

10. Bake the cake in the centre of the oven about 45 minutes, or until a skewer inserted in the centre comes out clean.

11. Allow to cool for 10 to 15 minutes. While the cake is still warm, place a plate over the top and invert the cake out of the pan onto the plate. Cover with a serving plate and invert again.

12. Serve warm or at room temperature with whipped cream, or just on its own.

Sunny-Side-Up Apricot Pastry

It's as fun to make and look at as it is to eat. This combination of buttery brioche dough, sweet vanilla pastry cream, and tart apricots masquerading as a sunny-side-up egg was made popular in Julia Child's book *Baking with Julia*.

Pastry cream is a staple in the pastry kitchen. To flavour this silky custard, you can use pure vanilla extract, or try a vanilla pod, which gives the most intense and satisfying flavour. If you have never had the opportunity to cook with a real vanilla pod, try it now and you'll be hooked. To use the pod, just slice it lengthwise with a paring knife to expose the seeds. Scrape the seeds out of the pod and throw the seeds and the pod into your saucepan. The pod will get strained out at the end, leaving the fragrant aroma and the flecks of real vanilla behind.

Makes eight 10cm/4in pastries.

The Pastry Cream
- 475ml/16 fl oz milk
- 90g/3½oz sugar
- 25g/1oz unsalted butter
- Pinch of salt
- ½ vanilla pod or 1 tsp pure vanilla extract
- 3 tbsp cornflour
- 1 egg
- 3 egg yolks

The Pastries
- 675g/1½lb (cantaloupe-size portion) Brioche dough (page 204)
- 225g/8oz pastry cream (above)
- 8 ripe apricots, halved (fresh in season or canned)
- 140g/5oz apricot jam, melted
- 400g/14oz sugar

For the Pastry Cream

1. Bring the milk, 50g/2oz of the sugar, butter, salt and vanilla pod to a gentle boil in a medium-to-large saucepan. Remove from the heat.

2. Whisk together the cornflour and the remaining sugar. Add the egg and egg yolks to the cornflour and mix into a smooth paste.

3. Slowly, and in small amounts, whisk a little of the hot milk into the egg mixture. Once the egg mixture is warm to the touch, pour it back into the milk in the pan.

4. Return the custard to the hob and bring to a boil, whisking continuously for 2 to 3 minutes until thickened.

5. Sieve the pastry cream into a shallow container and cover with clingfilm pressed directly on the surface to prevent a skin from forming.

6. Set the container in the freezer for 15 minutes, then refrigerate.

For the Pastries

7. Line a baking sheet with parchment paper or a silicone mat.

8. Dust the surface of the refrigerated dough with flour and cut off a cantaloupe-size piece. Dust the piece with more flour and quickly shape it into a rough ball by stretching the surface of the dough around to the bottom on all four sides, rotating the ball a quarter turn as you go.

9. Roll the dough to a 3mm/⅛in-thick rectangle, adding flour as needed to prevent sticking.

10. Cut out eight 10cm/4in circles, using a round pastry cutter. Save the scraps to use in Cinnamon Twists and Turns (page 244).

11. Cover the work surface with a generous coating of the sugar. Take one of the 4 rounds and lay it in the sugar. Using a rolling pin, roll back and forth over the centre, stopping 1cm/½in from the two ends to create an oval. If the dough sticks to the rolling pin, dust the rolling pin with a bit of flour. Lay the oval, sugar side up, on the lined baking sheet. Repeat with the rest of the dough, keeping the ovals at least 2.5cm/1in apart on the sheet.

12. Spread 2 tablespoons of the pastry cream in the centre of each sugared oval. Place 2 apricots over the pastry cream so they resemble sunny-side-up eggs. Rest the pastry for 45 minutes.

13. Thirty minutes before baking time, preheat the oven to 190°C/gas mark 5 (consider a longer preheat if you're finding your results to be denser than you like, see page 34). If you're not using a stone in the oven, 5 minutes is adequate. The stone is not essential when using a baking sheet.

14. Bake the pastries in the centre of the oven for about 35 minutes, or until the dough is golden brown and the sugar is nicely caramelised.

15. As soon as the pastries come out of the oven, brush the apricot jam over the apricots to give them a nice shine. Serve warm or cooled.

Blueberry Lemon Curd Ring

This wreath-shaped pastry showcases the bright flavours of fresh lemon and the sweetness ofsseason blueberries.

The delicious lemon curd is perfect for slathering on a hot piece of toast as well as for the filling of this pastry recipe.

Makes 1.

The Lemon Curd
• 6 egg yolks
• 200g/7oz sugar
• 120ml/4 fl oz lemon juice
• 1 tbsp lemon zest
• 115g/4oz unsalted butter, cut into 1cm/½ in slices

The Ring
• 675g/1½lb (cantaloupe-size portion) Brioche dough (page 204)
• 115g/4oz lemon curd
• 2 tbsp sugar
• 175g/6oz fresh blueberries
• Egg wash (1 egg beaten with 1 tbsp of water)
• Sugar for dusting the top

For the Lemon Curd

1. Whisk together all the ingredients except the butter in a large metal bowl.

2. Place the bowl over a pan of gently simmering water set up as a double boiler.

3. Stir constantly with a rubber spatula until the lemon curd begins to thicken, about 10 minutes.

4. Add the butter and continue to stir until it is completely melted and the curd is quite thick with a smooth consistency.

5. If there are any lumps, sieve the curd into a container; then cover with clingfilm and place in the freezer until cool. Then refrigerate.

For the Ring

6. Line a baking sheet with parchment paper or a silicone mat.

7. Dust the surface of the refrigerated dough with flour and cut off a cantaloupe-size piece. Dust the piece with more flour and quickly shape it into a ball by stretching the surface of the dough around to the bottom on all four sides, rotating the ball a quarter turn as you go.

8. Roll out the ball to a 3mm/⅛in-thick rectangle approximately 30 x 40cm/12 x 16in. As you roll out the dough, add flour as needed to prevent sticking.

9. Spread the lemon curd evenly over the dough. Sprinkle the berries over the lemon curd.

10. Starting with the long side of the dough, roll it up into a log. Join the two ends together to form a wreath shape; pinch together to seal. Place on the prepared baking sheet. Stretch the dough to make sure you have a nice wide opening in the middle of your wreath.

11. Make evenly spaced cuts all the way around the wreath about 4–5cm/1½–2in apart. The cuts should go nearly to the bottom of the dough but not all the way through, about 1cm/½in from the bottom of the log.

12. Fold every other cut piece out away from the centre. Allow the dough to rest for about 40 minutes (consider a longer rest time if you're finding your results to be denser than you like, see page 39).

13. Preheat the oven to 190°C/gas mark 5. Brush the dough with egg wash and generously dust with sugar.

14. Bake the ring in the centre of the oven for 35 to 40 minutes, or until golden brown and well set. Serve warm or cooled.

Plaited Raspberry Almond Cream Pastry

Although this is easy to put together, the end result is dramatic and impressive for a special brunch or coffee morning. If fresh raspberries are unavailable, it's a wonderful way to show off seasonal fruits like apples, pears, peaches and cherries.

Makes 1.

- 675g/1½lb (cantaloupe-size portion) Brioche dough (page 204)
- 115g/4oz almond cream (page 208)
- 140g/5oz raspberry jam
- 175g/6oz fresh raspberries
- Egg wash (1 egg beaten with 1 tbsp of water)
- Sugar for dusting the top

1. Line a baking sheet with parchment paper or a silicone mat.

2. Dust the surface of the refrigerated dough with flour and cut off a cantaloupe-size piece. Dust the piece with more flour and quickly shape it into a ball by stretching the surface of the dough around to the bottom on all four sides, rotating the ball a quarter turn as you go.

3. Roll out the dough into a 3mm/⅛in-thick rectangle. As you roll out the dough, add flour as needed to prevent sticking.

4. Lift the dough onto the lined baking sheet. Cover the centre third of the dough with the almond cream, the jam and the berries.

5. Using a pizza cutter, cut about twelve 1cm/½in wide strips down each side. Brush the strips lightly with egg wash. Fold the strips, left over right, criss-crossing over the filling. Lightly press the strips together as you move down the pastry, creating a plait. Allow the plait to rest for 40 minutes (consider a longer rest time if you're finding your results to be denser than you like, see page 39).

6. Preheat the oven to 190°C/gas mark 5. Brush the plait with egg wash and generously sprinkle with sugar.

7. Place the baking sheet in the centre of the oven. Bake the plait for 35 to 45 minutes, or until golden brown and bubbling. Serve warm.

Cinnamon Twists and Turns

This is a great recipe for left-over scraps of rolled-out Brioche dough. The end result may look a bit like modern art, but the flavour will be a real treat – wonderful with a cup of coffee.

- 90g/3½oz sugar
- 1 tbsp ground cinnamon
- Brioche dough or scraps
- Egg wash (1 egg beaten with 1 tbsp of water)

1. Line a baking sheet with parchment paper or a silicone mat.

2. Preheat the oven to 190°C/gas mark 5. If you're not using a stone in the oven, 5 minutes is adequate. The stone is not essential when using a baking sheet.

3. Mix the sugar and cinnamon together in a small bowl. Set aside.

4. Brush the surface of the brioche scraps very lightly with egg wash, and sprinkle generously with the cinnamon-sugar. Flip the dough over and repeat on the opposite side.

5. Using a pizza cutter, cut the dough into 2cm/¾in strips or leave the scraps in odd shapes. Twist the strips into spirals and space evenly on the baking sheet. Let them rest for 15 minutes. Depending on the size of the twists, they may turn in the oven and take on their own shape.

6. Bake for 15 to 20 minutes, or until golden brown. Serve warm.

Bread Pudding

Bread pudding is the ultimate comfort food. It is also the perfect use for the day-old bread you will have left over when making all the recipes in this book. We like to use slightly stale bread because it absorbs the custard so well. This is wonderful served with Kumquat Champagne Confit (page 247) when you want something decadent for brunch.

Makes 8 servings.

- 8 egg yolks
- 200g/7oz sugar
- 1 litre/1¾ pints single cream
- 3 tbsp rum or brandy (optional)
- 1 tsp vanilla extract
- ¼ tsp freshly grated nutmeg
- ¼ tsp ground cinnamon
- ½ tsp freshly grated orange zest
- 12 slices day-old bread, cut 1cm/½in thick
- 130g/4½oz raisins, optional

1. Preheat the oven to 160°C/gas mark 3.

2. In a large mixing bowl, whisk together the yolks, sugar, cream, rum, vanilla, nutmeg, cinnamon and zest until well combined.

3. Arrange the bread slices to fit nicely in a 20 x 30 x 5cm/8 x 12 x 2in baking dish. Sprinkle the raisins over the bread if using. Pour the custard slowly over the bread; let it sit for about 10 minutes. You may have to push the bread into the custard to guarantee no bread remains dry.

4. Cover loosely with foil, poking a few holes in the top to allow steam to escape. Place on the centre shelf in the oven. Bake for 1 hour, or until the centre is just firm.

5. Remove from the oven and allow to stand for 10 minutes. Serve warm with Kumquat Champagne Confit (page 247), and vanilla ice cream, if desired.

Kumquat Champagne Confit

This is a quick and tasty alternative to the more traditional marmalade recipe (page 114). It comes together very fast and packs an incredible flavour. We love this on fresh baguettes with a nice soft cheese like Brie or chèvre. It is also amazing as a topping for the Bread Pudding (page 246); just add a scoop of vanilla ice cream!

Makes 800g/1¾lb

- 200g/7oz sugar
- 475ml/16 fl oz champagne
- 250ml/8 fl oz water
- 1 star anise
- 25 kumquats, thinly sliced

1. In a medium-size saucepan, bring the sugar, champagne, water and star anise to a simmer. Cook, stirring until sugar has dissolved.

2. Add the kumquats and gently simmer over medium-low heat until they are tender and the liquid is the consistency of thick maple syrup, about 20 minutes.

3. Use within 1 week.

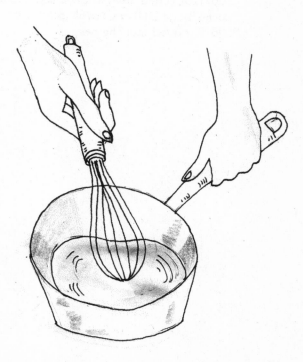

Chocolate Cherry Bread Pudding

'There is no end to the combinations of flavours you can use to make bread pudding. I first made this pudding with the Chocolate Bread (page 226). The intensity of the chocolate mixed with the tart cherries is a classic. It is also wonderful made with Brioche or Challah doughs. Served with a premium-quality vanilla ice cream, this dessert will satisfy any chocolate craving.' – Jeff

Makes 8 servings.

- 750ml/1¼ pints single cream
- 175g/6oz brown sugar
- 225g/8oz high-quality plain chocolate, preferably Valrhona or equivalent, finely chopped
- 50g/2oz butter, cut in 1cm/½in slices
- 3 whole eggs
- 2 egg yolks
- 350g/12oz cubed day-old Chocolate Bread (page 226), Brioche (page 204) or Challah (page 196)
- 250g/9oz dried sour cherries

1. Preheat the oven to 160°C/gas mark 3. Bring the cream and brown sugar to a simmer.

2. Remove from heat and add the chocolate and butter to the cream mixture, stirring until the chocolate is completely melted and smooth. Allow the mixture to cool slightly, about 5 minutes.

3. Whisk together the eggs and egg yolks and add to the cooled chocolate mixture.

4. Arrange the cubed bread and cherries in a 20 x 30 x 5cm/8 x 12 x 2in baking dish. Pour the chocolate custard over the bread and allow it to sit for 15 minutes. You may have to push the bread down into the custard to make sure it is well soaked.

5. Cover loosely with foil, poking a few holes in the top to allow steam to escape. Bake for about 50 minutes, or until the centre is firm to the touch.

6. Allow to sit for 10 minutes before serving with vanilla ice cream.

INDEX

ACKNOWLEDGEMENTS

Cookbook deals for unknown authors without TV shows are a long shot these days. On top of that, we knew bread baking, but we didn't know publishing. So we needed some luck, and some generous people to help us. Our most heartfelt thanks go to Ruth Cavin, our risk-taking editor at St. Martin's Press, who heard us on the radio, liked our idea, and decided to publish us. Decisive is good. Otherwise this would still be just an eccentric family project. Lynne Rossetto Kasper took Jeff's call on her radio show, which gave us the opportunity to meet Ruth. Lynne also gave great advice and connected us with our top-notch literary agent, Jane Dystel.

We also had great friends and family to act as recipe testers. They baked endlessly and shared their criticism and praise with us. Once they started using our recipes, we understood that this would be a book for everyone – avid bakers and non-bakers alike. That was a revelation. So we owe our book to them: Allison Campbell, Alex Cohn, Ralph Cohn, Shelly Fling, Paul Gates (whose home was the first proving ground), Ralph Gualtieri and Debora Villa (who carried our dough across international borders), Rachel Hertzberg and Julia Hertzberg (who proved that children could do our recipes), Jim and Theresa Murray, Lorraine Neal, Jennifer Sommerness and Laura Silver. In addition to testing the breads, experienced editors Allison, Shelly and Laura gave invaluable tips on the text itself. Thank you to Josh Manheimer, Dusti Kugler, Kelly Lainsbury, Craig Neal and Patricia Neal for lending their marketing expertise. Graham (Zoë's husband) gave us immeasurable moral support. And thanks to Fran Davis for allowing us to use nearly all the contents of her home as props for our photo shoots. Also thanks to Barb Davis for all of your support and to Laura Tiffany for opening your beautiful kitchen to us.

Gratitude to Zoë's colleagues from the culinary world who have served as mentors and shared their advice so generously: Stephen Durfee, Thomas Gumpel, Steven Brown, Raghavan Iyer, Suvir Saran and Andrew Zimmern.